AUSTRALIAN STORY

AUSTRALIAN STORY

BEHIND THE SCENES

FOREWORD BY CAROLINE JONES

Contents

Foreword

The minute he saw me he came over with his arms full of asparagus cans and tears in his eyes. I see him often, stacking the shelves at the supermarket. This time he could not wait to tell me how much he and his wife had got out of last night's *Australian Story*. 'That's exactly what it was like for us when she had the breast cancer. We knew just how those people felt.'

His face was alight with excitement, or perhaps with relief that somehow his family's experience had been represented last night on television, that their fear and pain had been acknowledged in public so that everyone could understand how hard it was and see the courage of the patients and their supporters.

'But what my wife really loved was the ladies taking up dragon-boat racing! She hadn't heard about that. Now she wants to do it too!'

We weren't alone for long. Nearby shoppers overheard us and came to join in, each with a favourite program. And there we were, an impromptu *Australian Story* club, between the pet food and the cereals, with many questions for me to answer about people who've been featured on the program over the years.

The stories and names tumbled out as though we knew them all quite well; as though we were at a school reunion, eager to catch up on news of old friends. It happens to me all the time. It doesn't get the shopping done but it does tell me that people find some sustaining quality in *Australian Story*, something of value which they remember and which they don't want to miss in the next program.

Our production manager Anita Atkins was touched by overhearing a conversation when she was on holiday, incognito, enjoying a tour of the spectacular Buchan Caves in Victoria. As the guide concluded the description and announced an imminent return to the bus, one tourist said to her companion, 'Oh thank goodness, we should be back at the motel in time to watch *Australian Story*.'

But why do people say 'We love it' and 'We never miss it'? Why do so many of the programs leave you with a sense of satisfaction and fulfilment?

Is it because, even unconsciously, we are learning something important from the person on the screen: how to survive or endure or remain hopeful, or even how to be happy?

I know I wonder, as I watch, how would I cope with that disgrace? Do I have that resilience, that patience, that capacity for forgiveness, that joy in just being alive?

This book gives you an insight into how these remarkable programs are made — how ordinary people are encouraged to lift the polite lid on life stories and disclose what really matters to them, with such unusual candour.

You'll read about how we find the stories; about the careful research needed to provide factual and visual content. You'll find out what it's like to be the subject of an *Australian Story*. To tell your story honestly is not easy. When you reveal not only your wins but what's gone wrong, you make yourself vulnerable to being judged and to loss of privacy. You are offering the generous gift of your own hard-won wisdom and that's invaluable because it's authentic. But because of the revelation involved and the mutual trust required, the going is seldom straightforward or simple.

You'll get a camera crew's perspective and that of the producer whose responsibility is to stay behind the camera. You'll read how each producer waits for the crisis of doubt which often comes part-way through the process and which must be patiently worked out before the subject can continue with confidence; how some stories have been several years in the making. When the shooting is complete, the film editor, with the producer must design an artistic way to structure the story and to present it with as much clarity, depth and detail as half-an-hour will allow. You'll get a sense of how arduous the production process is for all concerned, and how hilarious it can be at times.

Australian Story's success and longevity are largely due to the astute management and fine diplomacy of our Executive Producer, Deborah Fleming.

She is the first person you'll meet in this book. Don't be fooled when you read that she 'just directs the traffic'. She's the one who brings out the best in each of us and keeps the peace in a creative, competitive team. Her vision and stamina have kept this complex, demanding, high-wire act on the road for ten years, to present a fascinating mosaic of what it is to be Australian today.

In the pioneering era of white settlement in Australia, people made rugs by stitching together flour and sugar bags, scraps of worn suits and dresses and old woollen jumpers. This resourceful craft was born of poverty and thrift. Some of these bush rugs are family heirlooms now — endearing pieces of handiwork that tell a moving story of hard times and ingenuity.

So our Australian Stories weave together a tapestry of the tales of our country's people, in all their diversity. It's a patchwork rug, intricate in its complexity, with rough and smooth textures, made of light and very dark shades, a work of art and identity still in the making. What could be more warming for people than their stories: the memory of where they've come from, what they've made, what they've endured, how they've kept their faith in life? If this were not conserved, what framework of meaning would there be to sustain life and the continuity of culture?

The Aboriginal people have always understood that keeping the story alive is a crucial, sacred duty so that we know who we are and our place in the scheme of things. That is the tradition in which *Australian Story* stands and it's a pleasure to write this foreword because I believe whole-heartedly in the value of our endeavour.

This book invites you to come behind the scenes with us. It will make you an *Australian Story* insider.

Caroline Jones AO
Presenter *Australian Story*

Thereby Hangs a Tale

Deb Fleming

The *Australian Story* team have carted their cameras through the private domains of some of the nation's more intriguing people. From the Governor-General's residence at Yarralumla to the roadside grass that's home to itinerant 'Highway Man' John Cadoret, we've ploughed through hundreds of hectares of other people's personal space. We've drunk red wine at Chopper Read's Tasmanian farmhouse, wiped our feet on the Prime Minister's doormat at Kirribilli, wept with Wayne Bennett and giggled with Garry MacDonald.

We explain to people that we will monopolise a lot of their time and that the interviews will be long and thorough. But, like childbirth, no one appreciates the intensity of the experience until they're bang in the middle of it. On *Australian Story*, we prefer to film our 'subjects' in their home environment. We try not to break the best china, run over the dog or get mud on the carpets, but I have no doubt our hosts are euphoric when we finally pack up our lights, cameras and notebooks and melt into the dust.

When we ask people to appear on *Australian Story*, we are often asking them to forego the big dollars offered by commercial stations. The ABC is precluded by its own editorial guidelines from participating in chequebook journalism. We don't pay: it's as simple as that. So we're very grateful to those people who do leap off the cliff into our uncertain embrace with all the obvious risks involved. They really do put their lives in our hands. It continues to amaze us all that they do so — not least because most of us would find it difficult, if not impossible, to do the same.

A question I'm often asked is: what is it like to work on *Australian Story*? As executive producer, I supervise a team of eight producers and two researchers, along with camera crews and editors who technically work for a different department of the ABC but who are assigned to *Australian Story*.

Tim Sharp, a young Brisbane artist who featured in an *Australian Story* episode in 2004, turned his imagined version of the team's various roles into a drawing which now hangs on our office wall. I'm portrayed as an evil harridan in some kind of control tower, brandishing a mobile phone in one hand and a cannon in the other, bellowing instructions to cowering and stressed-out subordinates. The producer of Tim's story, Kris Taylor, obviously provided a lurid account of the interpersonal dynamics of the place!

If I were the one applying paint to canvas, I'd probably portray myself as a frantic traffic cop. I'm the one who stands in the middle of the road, breathing in other people's exhaust fumes, dodging semi trailers and holding up the stop/go signs. I try to keep the traffic moving, I deal with the occasional road rage incident and I struggle to avert minor prangs and head-on collisions. I am ready to administer CPR at a moment's notice.

But the sad truth is that even a day on a traffic island would constitute an exciting excursion. An executive producer's job is office-bound. In colloquial terms, I am the hirer and firer of the staff, I commission the stories and I have the final say on what goes to air and in what form. The producers are the ones who are actually out there 'on the road', and they're busy people, each juggling four roles: researching, producing, reporting and directing the stories. None of them have psychology degrees but all have become skilled observers of the human psyche in all its complexity.

'To see ourselves as others see us...' an average day at Australian Story mission control through the eyes of Brisbane artist Tim Sharp.

For me, the computer and the phone are my lifeline to all the exciting things happening as the stories are filmed. I have three phones on my desk and they ring all day, usually with problems and bad news. Someone's threatening to sue. Someone's fallen out with his or her story producer. Someone's developed an unreciprocated romantic attachment to his or her story producer. Someone's changed their mind about telling their story. And always, always the money hassles that come with trying to make the best possible programs on a budget that is small by industry standards.

But sometimes that irritating ring-ring signals good news — very good news. This most often takes the form of a story, long pursued, that has finally fallen across the line. These are the 'big ones' and there is no denying the adrenalin rush that arrives with them.

Over the years, the greeting 'Deb, it's Mara' has often been the precursor of something special. Mara Blazic is our Melbourne-based senior researcher/associate producer and a certain inflexion in her voice is usually the giveaway: a deliberate restraint and flatness in the phrasing, indicating suppressed excitement. With these three words Mara has announced such scoops as our revealing story on Professor Alan Fels (chairman of the ACCC); Kerry Packer's helicopter pilot, Nick Ross, talking for the first time about donating a kidney to his boss; and, this year, cricketer David Hookes' girlfriend breaking her silence about his death.

In the Brisbane office, researcher Kristine Taylor famously opened the door for an *Australian Story* interview that really did change history; Helen Grasswill's encounter in 2002 with then Governor-General Dr Peter Hollingworth. Superior research is the foundation of all our most powerful stories.

How did it all begin?

In a way, you could say *Australian Story* started with the ABC satire *Frontline*, which mercilessly laid bare the vanities and hypocrisies of television journalism — and not just the tabloid variety. Some of us were working on the *7.30 Report* then and we identified ourselves in a new, unflattering light. (Eight years later, it was *Australian Story*'s turn to become an object of satire when the ABC's CNNNN team cuttingly characterised it as 'Award Winning Misery'. We really knew we'd made it when that happened.)

The *7.30 Report* mailbag and phone log were sending an unequivocal message that the audience was weary of what we were delivering back in 1995: 'Wake up to yourselves'; 'Get real'; 'I won't be watching any more'. It hurt. We finally grasped that they were wise to our tricks and were sick of reporters and of relentless confrontation.

Some of us also had a vague sense that something worthwhile was falling through the grating as a result of television's persistent and reductionist typecasting of individuals into heroes or villains. There's a phrase that had some currency in BBC news and current affairs at one time: the bias against understanding. Its use then, as I remember, related to the perceived need to provide the audience with more background and context in order to better understand complex and unfolding news stories. But perhaps it was also applicable to stories covered in a one-dimensional way, or from a particular ideological point of view. What was being lost was all the fascinating complexity and ambiguity of the human experience; the shades of grey and the colours of contradiction. The stuff of Shakespeare, no less.

We eventually got the chance to put this approach into practice with *Australian Story*, tackling a range of topics and interviewing people some of our peers loudly disapproved of: Philip Ruddock (when he was Immigration Minister); Pauline Hanson; Chopper Read; the disgraced Pan Pharmaceuticals founder Jim Selim. We felt there was no one who should be intrinsically and automatically out of bounds; but if we were to tackle them, we would have to pass our own test of extracting honest responses and genuinely adding to the sum of public knowledge and the wider spectrum of media coverage. This approach attracted howls of anger at times — and certainly some of our efforts were more successful than others — but we embarked on all these projects with open minds, intense curiosity and a genuine sense of journalistic inquiry.

The chance to start setting some of our ideas in motion came in 1995 when Paul Williams, a veteran of *A Big Country*, *Four Corners* and *Lateline*, was appointed Director of News and Current Affairs in Sydney. Paul had some bold ideas he wanted to implement. First, he wanted to strengthen the *7.30 Report* by centralising it. At the time it was produced separately out of the individual states, so his suggestion was certain to be controversial. So, as part of the overall package to be presented to the ABC Board, he proposed a new program tentatively titled *Australian Correspondent*. It would have a particular emphasis on regional Australia, be an hour long and go to air at seven thirty on Saturday nights.

A subsequent paper prepared for the Board described it like this:

> *Australian Correspondent* will carry stories about the people, the issues and the changing social fabric of regional Australia — stories that have largely disappeared from the small screen ... However it will project a contemporary image, illuminating all facets of Australia's culturally diverse way of life ... The program will cater to our audience's intense curiosity about other people's lives ...

So how did I end up getting involved? When Paul, all bush bonhomie and RM Williams boots said, 'So what do you reckon — would you like to be the executive producer of *Australian Correspondent?*'

At the time, I was executive producer (EP) of the Queensland edition of *7.30 Report*. I had moved back to Brisbane after stints in Sydney as a senior producer on Channel Nine's *Today* show and EP of the *7.30 Report* in Sydney. Paul's offer was like winning the lottery. It was also totally terrifying. I had never developed a new program from the ground up, but I could hardly refuse the gleaming gift I had just been handed. I remember feeling a huge weight of responsibility and gratitude, and an intense determination not to let him down.

Supervising producer Patricia Barraclough was coerced and cajoled — conned, I am sure she would say — into moving to Brisbane from Canberra to be an equal partner in this exciting new enterprise. Production manager Anita Atkins was poached from the

ABC Queensland newsroom much to the distress of her colleagues there, deprived at a stroke of her efficiency and equilibrium.

It should not pass without comment that Paul's decision to situate the show in Brisbane was revolutionary. At that time, and for many years subsequently, no prime time programs on any network were based out of anywhere other than Sydney or Melbourne. Paul might just as well have chosen to locate the show in Botswana, so eccentric did the decision seem to some.

Fast forward to mid-February 1996. The staff — many of them drawn from the collapsed state editions of the *7.30 Report* — were due in Brisbane for a big weekend workshop to discuss the new program. Paul Williams would be there to talk to us, as would several other major industry figures, lined up by Tricia whose industry contacts are unparalleled. These guest speakers included writer and filmmaker Tony Maniaty, *Four Corners* legend Chris Masters and distinguished documentary-maker Mike Rubbo.

Paul arrived in Brisbane on the eve of the big weekend looking uncharacteristically grim. 'Bad news, gang,' he said. A harsh new financial climate was descending. Our program would have to adapt or perish. Instead of a one-hour program in a weekend time slot, we were required to morph into a half-hour show at 8 pm, mid-week.

Tricia Barraclough and I went pale, took several deep breaths and started scribbling frantically on bits of paper, trying to design a new show in the few hours that remained before morning. Deepening the horror was the knowledge that we had to face our expectant team — and our guest stars — at the workshop with some sort of coherent game plan.

Thinking back to that time now, I am reminded of Clementine Churchill's words to her husband, British Prime Minister Winston Churchill, when he realised he had lost the general election after of World War II. 'You know, this

The gang of three, 1996. Trying to look cool and focused for a news article. Left to right: Supervising Producer Patricia Barraclough, Executive Producer Deborah Fleming and Director David Gunzburg.

may be a blessing in disguise,' she reportedly ventured. To which Churchill is said to have responded: 'In that case, it is certainly very well disguised.' In our case, what seemed a disaster was indeed a blessing, because it blasted us in a more radical direction than we had ever intended.

In the morning, we presented the results of our febrile overnight deliberations to our shell-shocked troops. Thank God for the wisdom and eloquence of our guests, Messrs Maniaty, Masters and Rubbo, who challenged, educated and inspired our team to embrace the new format and kick-started the process of opening our eyes to some better ways to tell stories.

I still remember Tony Maniaty's comments on the lack of storytelling in most television programs: 'We only have to look at the plethora of TV current affairs and news and infotainment shows — and apply the most basic rules of storytelling to them — to see how sadly lacking they are. Current affairs programs these days have very little to do with good storytelling and more to do with misanthropy. They've become a kind of nightly blood sport for bored office workers … These shows are not about real conflicts and real people. They do not touch their audiences; they do not come within cooee of evoking passionately the universal truths. Things like loyalty, betrayal, love, honour, justice.'

What came out of that conference was our determination to search out the human dramas and conflicts underpinning everyday experiences. We would not be concentrating on politics and economics but on the broad sweep of 'meaning of life' issues that affect human happiness. Our new economy-version program would feature three stories with very little reporter narration and certainly none of those ubiquitous 'stand-ups' or 'pieces to camera'.

The next step was to start making the stories and, in particular, a pilot or demo program. One element that we had in place from the beginning was the very best camera and sound operators and tape editors in the business. Anthony Sines, Laurence McManus, Ian Harley, Roger Carter and Kent Gordon were founding members of the team, and all of us owe them a great deal. Anthony, Ian, Roger and Kent are still with us, now joined by Angela Trabucco, and Laurence remains a regular contributor. (Quentin Davis, Ross Byrne and Marc Smith were later recruits and have built on the tradition.)

Sparkling pictures, sound and editing gave us a distinctive edge from the outset, so even if those of us on the editorial side were flailing around — and we were — the look of the stories was stunning and distinctive.

The first completed story was on former RSL President Sir William Keys and his use of Chinese traditional medicine in his battles with cancer. Put together by Phil Williams — a great film-maker and storyteller — the piece was powerful, distinctive and moving.

But much as we loved the story, something wasn't quite right. It was our director, David Gunzburg who put his finger on it: there was too much reporter narration. There were actually only four short lines of narration, but David said, 'Get Keys to say the same thing in his own words and you will have a story told entirely by him. It will be much more powerful.'

He was right. We did just that, and it was a big turning point for the show.

In the midst of getting the stories right, there were some other big issues we had to attend to. Like finding a presenter. And finding a title.

Australian Correspondent no longer fitted a truncated half-hour show with invisible reporters. We toyed with *Southern Cross*, but someone in South Africa had already registered the name. One of our producers, Ges d'Souza, I think, suggested *Australian Story*. We didn't immediately love it, but it wasn't bad. It stuck.

The presenter issue was trickier. Should we even have

Sleeping on the job? Producer Caitlin Shea and Editor Roger Carter share a rare relaxed moment during a story edit.

one? After all, we were effectively abandoning traditional reporters. Tricia Barraclough and I were torn.

We were both big admirers of Caroline Jones and, if we were going to have a presenter, she would be ideal. She had a long and distinguished history as an ABC journalist and broadcaster in TV and radio. More recently, on her ground-breaking Radio National show, *The Search for Meaning*, she had pioneered what has since become known as the confessional style of interviewing. (In a development that was to have significant echoes for *Australian Story* down the track, Caroline's program was axed for being 'too soft'. Her ABC bosses wanted her interviews to be more confrontational, perhaps missing the point that people were actually revealing a lot more than many adversarial interviews achieve. The point was seemingly not lost on people like Andrew Denton. When Denton launched his new interview show some years later, he called it *Enough Rope*. Enough said.)

Caroline flew up to Brisbane to meet us. Caroline has a daunting reputation, beautiful manners and is, of course, a picture of elegance. But she can dazzle with ribald blasts of wit and wicked humour. She is not just an entertaining talker; she is a world-class listener with finely honed intuition and empathy. A rarity in a superficial business. We were desperate to involve her in the project and, thankfully, she was interested and always encouraging.

In the end, we opted for a compromise. Caroline agreed to join us as a contributor, ambassador and presenter of some episodes. But we would regularly use 'guest introducers' as well, to provide elements of freshness and surprise. These, in due course, ranged from a former US President, to the Australian Prime Minister, to movie stars Nicole Kidman and Russell Crowe.

Just before Easter in 1996 we completed a three-item pilot program and despatched it to the bosses in Sydney with our hearts in our mouths.

Within twenty-four hours, the feedback was flashing back to Brisbane. It was good. There were some excited phone calls and reports that our tape was generating 'goose bumps' as it was passed from office to office all around ABC HQ at Gore Hill.

Somehow, out of all our doubt and chaos, we had delivered something stirring.

The well-received pilot program was essentially what went to air on 29 May 1996 as *Australian Story*, Episode One. We watched the broadcast over a few drinks in the office and, as the end credits rolled, waited hopefully for the congratulatory feedback. We were to be disappointed. The reaction from press, public and peers was muted — definitely more a whimper than a bang. No sign that anyone had sighted the 'Storming of the Bastille' but no waves of condemnation either. Ratings were OK: neither spectacularly good nor bad.

There was satisfaction in the fact that the program was at least original and not, like most 'new' Australian television programs, a slavish carbon copy of an American or British formula.

Encouragingly, there were a number of unusually warm, articulate and enthusiastic faxes and emails from viewers. We kept all of them, pressed into a scrapbook, and we still refer back to them sometimes.

Time then to settle in, let people get used to us and start finding and telling some ripping yarns …

Australian Story was on its way. We gradually evolved from two or three stories per episode to only one, and experimented with running stories over consecutive weeks. We encountered four changes of time slot and a couple of near axings. We survived Jonathon Shier and an attempt to move us out of the News and Current Affairs Department — a move that would have been fatal in my view. We have enjoyed consistent support from our bosses in News Caff through all the vicissitudes of the last decade. We won our first Walkley Award (one of journalism's most prestigious) in 1997, our second year, for 'Valentine's Day', a story by Ben Cheshire and Sophie Emtage about a heroin addict. Several more Walkleys followed in subsequent years.

The Sandra Levy-inspired move to Mondays at 8 pm in 2000 proved to be inspired indeed, and turned out to be a natural home for us. Our audience grew each successive year.

One criticism of *Australian Story* that has persisted over the years is the view that the program is 'soft' and lacking rigour; that we simply let our interviewees say whatever they wish, without challenging or testing them. *The Australian*'s Matt Price could always be relied upon to exert deflationary pressure on swelled egos. We were as 'soft as a choc stick melting in the midday sun,' he said. On another occasion he called us 'downright dodgy'. Then there was the senior ABC colleague who said on radio that politicians only ever received two opportunities for a 'free kick': one was via the *Women's Weekly*, the other was on *Australian Story*. Ouch.

Producer John Millard. John left the ABC this year. He made a big contribution to Australian Story on all levels.

Let me set the record straight now. The research and preparation for an *Australian Story* piece is painstaking and thorough. Most of our main interviews run for several hours and, as interviewees will testify, they can be exhausting and exhaustive. Viewers can be confident the research has been done and the hard questions have been asked; it's just that generally you don't hear the questions, only the answers — although occasionally a question will be included in the broadcast if it is essential to understand the answer. We don't ambush our subjects but they are told our overarching responsibility is to tell a fair and truthful story.

The letters and emails we receive from people who watch the show demonstrate that we have a very discerning audience. We delight in their ability to read between the lines and draw their own conclusions.

Increasingly, our viewers are also providing the ideas that actually make it to air. Twenty-five per cent of our stories started that way in 2004. We are ever more in their debt!

Selecting my favourite *Australian Story* pieces is like choosing between children or picking out a puppy at an RSPCA refuge. It involves a cornucopia of conflicting emotions.

One piece that always comes to mind is Helen Grasswill's breakthrough in 1996 when she coaxed Rupert Murdoch's longtime right-hand man and then News Ltd chief Ken Cowley on camera. It was a revealing and emotional story, and Cowley was our first 'high-profile' interviewee. No doubt this helped open the door a little wider for those that followed.

During the 2001 election we presented a matching pair of 'In the Family' profiles of leaders Kim Beazley and John Howard. The stories were controversial at the time and much debated. Like so much about *Australian Story*, however, there were elements of accident about the way those stories happened. We set out initially, some time before the election, to prepare a profile of John and Janette Howard. Producer Wendy Page eventually persuaded the notoriously media-shy Mrs Howard to appear on camera. That process took some months, and by the time she had consented the country was in pre-election mode. The ABC has strict guidelines on editorial balance and these apply with special rigour during elections. It rapidly became apparent that there should be a 'balancing' profile of the Beazley family.

It is practically unheard-of for a politician to deliberately shove a camera out of the way with an election looming. But when we approached Mr Beazley's office it was clear the ALP leader was not inclined to cooperate with us immediately. He was aware that the project with the Howards had been underway for some months. Time and access had been very limited, of course, and there wasn't a great deal 'in the can', but Mr Beazley's staff weren't to know that. They wanted to know why their boss was 'not receiving equal time and consideration'. It was all very awkward because, in the climate of an election, we couldn't run our exclusive material with the Howards without some equivalent from the Beazleys. Thankfully, several interventions later, Mr Beazley agreed to participate and he and his wife, Suzie, were good-humoured and patient as were the Howards.

In my opinion, the two 'In the Family' episodes were interesting and insightful, but subtle; very much in the *Australian Story* tradition of inviting the audience to arrive at their own judgements. I felt in both episodes we achieved our stated aim of 'adding to the spectrum of public knowledge about a significant individual or issue'. One academic suggested on radio that 'these

Australian Story profiles were so valuable, they should become a regular part of the ABC's election coverage'.

On another front, producer Wendy Page set out to explore the far edges of the format and successfully took us into the investigative arena. Among other stories, she put together a series of programs that explored the legacy of the crimes of serial killer Eric Edgar Cooke in Western Australia.

The first story featured Cooke's son, high profile trade union leader Tony Cooke who had never before spoken on national television about his notorious father. The final episode brought together the Cooke family, the family of a young woman murdered by Cooke and the family of the man wrongly imprisoned for the murder of the young woman. In 2002 Wendy and editor/director Ian Harley received a very well deserved Walkley Award for the story.

Few who were involved will ever forget the eye-of-the-storm experience when our story on Governor-General Dr Peter Hollingworth became THE story. A couple of days after broadcast, our methods were placed under unprecedented public scrutiny during the furore that erupted when Dr Hollingworth indicated he felt he had been misrepresented by us in the editing process in relation to his remarks about a fourteen-year-old girl and her relationship with a priest. We were forced — for the first time and with great reluctance — to publicly release camera tape 'rushes' and transcripts of unedited interview material. The unanimous view of the press commentators and the public, on the basis of this evidence, was that the Governor-General had been fairly represented. It was a tough few days though, and a salutary reminder of what it is like to be on the receiving

Strike a pose. Cameraman Anthony Sines in the middle of a Tom Cruise moment.

end of rabid media scrutiny. Producer Helen Grasswill and the team had been working with little or no sleep to turn the story around at great speed and it would have been all too easy for unintended error to creep in. So it's a credit to all involved that editorial accuracy and integrity were maintained and the end product survived the intense scrutiny it received at that time from the press and public.

Vanessa Gorman and Pip Quinn's episode on Brisbane Broncos' coach Wayne Bennett is always high on my list if I am asked about favourite episodes. It was a perfect *Australian Story* in my eyes, with all the elements that could be wished for: drama; conflict; surprises; newsworthiness; immediacy; intensely moving and engaging. It never won any awards — like so many really good stories, it seemed to defy the categorisation required by awards committees — but the accolades rolled in from all quarters and have never really stopped rolling. In fact, we loved it so much we repeated it at every opportunity until the poor Bennett family had to beg us to desist. Nevertheless, our audience has never tired of it and we still get requests for re-runs. Our two Logie award - winning stories; one on Hazel Hawke and the other about the Milat family linger in memory too.

There are so many other stories and individuals richly deserving of mention but time and space do not permit.

It's perhaps enough just to say that all of us on *Australian Story* still get excited by the stories we hear and those we get a chance to tell. Paul Williams once asked me if I thought we would run out of stories. I can't remember what I replied then, but if I was asked now I would say, 'Not a chance.'

Life really is stranger than fiction and the stories that come across our desks provide endless fascination. There are days when you just can't wait to catch up with the latest twist in an episode being filmed or researched; or to view videotape footage as it arrives back in the office. 'Come and look at this,' someone shouts and we all gather, riveted, in front of the monitor.

It was British clergyman and writer Charles Caleb Colton (1780–1832) who said 'Imitation is the sincerest form of flattery', and Percy Bysshe Shelley (1792–1822) who claimed that 'Imitation is the strongest force for moral good'. It is now nearly ten years since *Australian Story* made its first tentative appearance and while the airwaves may not be awash with moral good, they are flowing with a certain amount of flattery of the Caleb Colton kind.

We always envisaged *Australian Story* as being part of the tradition of current affairs reporting. We just wanted to try another approach which we hoped would illuminate issues and individuals in a different way. We don't see our path as a rejection of the adversarial, investigative method, but as a supplement to it.

But there is evidence that we have had a big influence. On the ABC, in conventional current affairs programs, on commercial channels and even in print, our contemporaries are proudly telling stories 'Oz Story-style'. The market we once had all to ourselves has become very crowded indeed.

I do not see that as a problem but as a vindication of our experiment. We took a big risk and we continue to take that risk, week by week.

Behind the scenes, our first ten years have been tough, harrowing and relentless. I have enjoyed them immensely.

On the beach. The team at Noosa for an end of year Christmas party.

The Bennetts at home. Left to right: Trish, Catherine, Elizabeth, Justin and Wayne.

A Man For All Seasons

Vanessa Gorman

He was the highly successful Rugby League coach of the Brisbane Broncos, but Wayne Bennett was also the most guarded and private of public figures. His disdain for the media was legendary.

In May 1999, *Australian Story* revealed the man behind the mask. His extraordinary story of hardship and courage was a revelation that made grown men weep.

'Who's Wayne Bennett?'

Researcher Phillipa Quinn eyed me with a look part exasperation, part horror. She was spruiking me a hard-won story she had been chasing for twelve months, but her triumph in securing Bennett's cooperation was suddenly deflated by the ignorant producer standing before her.

'The Brisbane Broncos' coach,' she said. 'Arguably the best Rugby League coach in the country.'

I felt myself recoil. I had been raised just north of the Victorian border, where AFL was the code. I knew next to nothing about Rugby League and, if the truth be known, had no interest in finding out. As producers and journalists we are often asked to wrap our minds around unfamiliar subjects but this one seemed so far out of my comfort zone I was determined to sidestep it altogether.

'Maybe it'd be best if a bloke did it. Ben would do a good job.'

'I know what you're thinking,' Phillipa said, 'but it's not just a football story. He's had an incredibly tough life and has made a success of things despite that. And he has two children who are disabled.'

Courage under adversity, human hardship — these were subjects within my comfort zone. 'OK, so tell me more,' I said, still a little wary but warming to the idea.

I began reading about the public Wayne Bennett, a figure who seemed to embody the term 'enigma'. Notoriously wary of the media, hostile even; packing up his kit bag and refusing to talk when he didn't like the way the press dealt with something. While he was obviously loved by his players and engendered fierce loyalty, the face he showed the world was that of a sullen, monosyllabic, intimidating sourpuss. This will be interesting, I thought. At best a challenge; at worst something akin to pulling teeth.

Wayne Bennett's success as both player and coach was on the public record. During the 1980s he co-coached the Canberra Raiders, helping the club reach the NSW Rugby League Grand Final for the first time. The Brisbane Broncos were formed in 1988 and Wayne was chosen as inaugural coach. Both his rise and that of the club was meteoric, on what had now become a national stage.

The Broncos won the Grand Final in 1992, 1993, 1997 and 1998, and would go on to win again in 2000. When Wayne was coach for the Queensland team, they won the State of Origin series in 1987, 1988, 1998 and 2001.

Australian Story researcher Phillipa Quinn, a Broncos fan, had seen Wayne carrying his disabled daughter Catherine up the stairs of the stands on match day. She'd also heard about his son, Justin, but had no idea of the extent of his disability. Like most of the sports journalists, she knew there was another story to tell but, to their credit, the media had always respected Wayne's wish to keep his children out of the limelight so they could grow and be themselves without exposure or pressure. They had never filmed Catherine at matches or Justin when he came with Wayne to training. Both Wayne and his wife, Trish, felt they would not be ready to share their family story until the children left school, which had happened not long before Phillipa came to me with the story.

We were concerned Wayne might tend towards the monosyllabic character we knew from the press room after the game.

A media liaison officer at the Broncos made the first approach to Wayne about our request to film an *Australian Story* on his life and family. In typical candid fashion Wayne later admitted knowing nothing about the program.

> I checked the TV programs, saw it come on, watched it one night, thought they did that pretty well. I have about one friend in the media so I rang him and I asked him about Australian Story and what he thought and he said, 'I would do it if I was you because they will do it properly.' He said, 'They won't sensationalise it, they won't abuse your position,' and that kind of fell into line with what I wanted to do. I wanted to do the story and, I gotta say, they were pretty smart the ABC. They brought Vanessa in, somebody out of town who didn't have a football background.

Not having a football background was both a help and a handicap. What I was rapidly getting a background on, however, was the extent of Wayne's fearsome reputation with the media. His disdain for them was legendary and I began to feel those first flutters of trepidation in the pit of my stomach. If he could intimidate the hoariest of hard-nosed sports journos, what could he do to a football ignoramus like myself?

Even then, I didn't realise exactly how scared I should have been. My ignorance afforded me a little bliss. The first time Phillipa took me to Wayne's house to introduce me to him and his family, I still had no idea I was about to meet someone who sports journalist Roy Masters would describe as standing just below (coach) Jack Gibson, 'which is somewhere just above God'.

Instead of the ogre I was expecting, the man I met was polite and friendly. I came to realise much later that when Wayne decides to do something, he gives it his heart and soul.

I came clean about my own shortcomings as a follower of Rugby League in general and his career in particular. He didn't seem to mind and hauled out a couple of boxes of musty archives: newspaper articles chronicling his career, old photo albums, the paraphernalia of a life. God love him, I thought; this was going to make my job a little easier.

It's one of the unusual privileges of being a producer on *Australian Story*: to front up to someone's house and delve into their emotional, personal, public and spiritual lives. To be given permission to peruse scrapbooks and photo albums, to pry into the corners of their past. I never took this privilege for granted, and always tried to repay it with a sensitivity to the difficult task we were inviting our subjects to undertake — sharing their private life on national television.

'If it helps only one person then that's a good enough reason to do it,' said Wayne.

Trish Bennett welcomed us with her customary warmth and introduced their daughters, Elizabeth, 21, and Catherine, 18. Catherine was manoeuvring about the house in her motorised wheelchair. Their son, Justin, 22, was cheerful and affectionate and invited us to see his extensive football jersey collection. At first I sensed a reticence in the girls about the possibility of a story, but things thawed over afternoon tea. Phillipa had related to me her experience of meeting the family for the first time a few weeks previously, when she'd felt as if she was the one being interviewed and auditioned instead of the other way around. She must have passed muster: she came on board as an associate producer, taking the crew off on weekends to film the Broncos' early matches.

It was the beginning of the 1999 Rugby League season and the Broncos were fresh from two consecutive Grand Final wins. This was to be a story about a man who had been through hardships but now was riding high in his career, we decided. A man who was enjoying the success of being part of a winning team. Except, to our alarm, that's not how things began to unfold. The Broncos lost their first two matches.

An early-season hiccup we reasoned and set about filming Wayne's early life.

Our first shooting trip took us to the small town of Allora near Warwick in south-east Queensland. Wayne showed us the house he'd lived in, next door to his grandparents' house, and began to talk about his father, Jim, a fettler on the railways. A drinker and a gambler, Jim made things hard for the family. Wayne recalled how they would hide under the bed when people came knocking to collect monies owed — money Jim had invariably spent on drink or gambling.

Wayne's mother, Patsy, remembered how Jim 'came home real drunk and kicked us all out of our beds and tore all our sheets and blankets in half and we'd suffered in the freezing cold of a Warwick winter …'

His sister Michelle cried during the interview when she recalled the hard times Patsy had endured raising the four children. She left home at five thirty every morning to make breakfast in the local hotel. 'We did get bagged. We were bagged heavily in Warwick. We were the Bennett kids and we were nothing and we were nobodies and I don't think any of us have forgotten that.'

Walking the streets of his childhood town nowadays with Wayne Bennett, it was a different story. People came out of stores to welcome home the conquering hero, his status as social outcast a distant memory. Something in Wayne's face told me that while he had forgiven the people who had once looked down on the family, he hadn't forgotten. But, in what I was to discover was typical Bennett fashion, after walking the hardest of roads he had fashioned the noblest of paths.

> As I grew into adulthood I just made sure that I never looked down on anybody, regardless of their situation. Because I knew what I'd experienced and I didn't think anyone had the right to do that, and because I think it's really important to me to treat everybody fairly, regardless of who's your dad, what your background is, whether you've got great wealth or you're just a battler. It's what you've got to offer that's important to me and I don't care about your background.

Many people have lived through great adversity in childhood. What is it that makes one person go off the rails and another determined to succeed against all odds? This is the enigma of the human spirit that we, as filmmakers and storytellers, are constantly trying to decipher. In Wayne Bennett's case I sensed it was the love he felt for his family that sent him down the road he was to travel. As much as his father was irresponsible, Wayne wanted to be responsible. With a drunk for a father, he made a promise to his mother that he wouldn't drink; a promise not given lightly in a town where a few beers after work or footy was the main social pastime.

'I didn't drink because I didn't want to let her down,' he said. 'I didn't want to cause her more worry.'

It was his only way to thank his mother for the sacrifices she had made. As Wayne's younger brother, Bob, told us: 'I had an older brother that was smart and made good decisions, and I followed his decisions and I didn't drink and I didn't smoke and I didn't gamble, and that was all because Wayne didn't do it.'

There it was early in Wayne Bennett's life: the grit, the steely determination, that would carry him out of poverty and hopeless circumstances and help him make something extraordinary of his life.

Filming for *Australian Story* can take you to places that leave you breathless with awe and wonder. Alternatively, they can take you to an abattoir in Warwick on a cold autumn morning.

Wayne was eleven when his father left home. At thirteen he was forced to leave school and begin work as a gut boy in the Warwick bacon factory. Showing the resolve and determination that would become a hallmark of his life, Wayne set himself the task of getting into the police force. His sister Michelle recalled, 'That was a very big thing for us because we'd been nothings and we'd been nobodies. And you just didn't get into the police force with what we call our credentials.'

Wayne failed the entrance exam dismally the first time around, but was accepted as a cadet in 1966 and sworn into the Queensland police force in 1969. He was also a talented footballer and represented Queensland from 1971–73 and played for Australia on the 1971 tour of New Zealand.

But it was as a football coach that Wayne would find his true vocation, embodying the necessary combination of disciplined trainer, father figure, strategist and mentor.

As player Kevin Walters told us: It's not so much how many teams he's coached to victories or how many premierships he's won, I think it's more what he's done with the young men who have come to the club. He makes sure when they leave the club they are better people, and I know he's been very successful at that.

Filming Wayne at training, in the dressing rooms at matches or around the club, it was obvious to us that he took very seriously his responsibilities to the young men from all over the state. At the time, players from other clubs had been running amok, bringing the game into disrepute. It was clear that such behaviour would not be tolerated at the Broncos. Wayne had worked hard to create a culture at the club that was family-based and even the older players looked upon him as a father figure. Captain Allan

Langer added that he also classed Wayne as one of his best friends.

There was still more to this story, though. Wayne had made a success of the police force and a success of football, but then life had dealt him another succession of blows. I just wasn't sure how much he would open up to us in an interview about his personal life.

The *Australian Story* interview is a complex piece of work. As viewers know, the interview not only tells but also drives and shapes the story. There's no voice-over adding spin or filling in the gaps. One person's experience or life story is retold by various voices, with archival and actual sound adding texture and information. Often people are speaking about painful or difficult memories and emotions, private experiences that are still raw. As producers we try to provide a safe space for people to talk. We spend weeks in their lives, building rapport and understanding, establishing their trust that we are not out to do a job on them but to tell their story with the utmost integrity.

Sometimes our main interview can take hours to record and it's hard to predict how someone will cope with that. I was concerned Wayne might tend towards the monosyllabic character we knew from the press room after a game. I needn't have worried. Here was a man who had thought deeply about his life and others', who was conscious of his motives, knew both where he had come from and where he was going, and lived by a highly developed moral code. He revealed himself as a complex person who had struggled against all odds to live a life of achievement and integrity, who had been struck down by life's blows more than once but had a deep acceptance of the things he couldn't change. I was amazed at Wayne's eloquence and his openness about the private corners of his life, and a number of times I was wrestling with my own tears as he spoke.

When the Bennetts' son, Justin, was twelve months old an immunisation needle sent him into convulsions, causing severe brain damage. Wayne recalled being summoned from the oval one afternoon and driving to the hospital with a heavy heart to find his baby son severely ill. Seventeen months later their daughter Elizabeth was born healthy, and three years after that Catherine arrived. Catherine was born with severe physical deformities.

'The doctor came out when I was in the waiting room. He said, "Wayne, things aren't real good. We haven't got a good one here." Funny how you remember the exact words. Well, I went in and I can still see her lying there now. She was just a mangled mess.'

Wayne told a story that has always stayed with me but which we weren't able to include in the episode due to time constraints. Catherine was to be born by caesarean. The night before, the Bennetts were in hospital with another couple who looked, Wayne remembered, 'like they'd done it pretty tough'.

The nurse asked the husband where she could find him once the baby was born.

> And he said, 'Oh, I'll be at one of the ponderosas.' And I'm thinking, ponderosa, what's he talking about, this guy? She said, 'What do you mean ponderosa, Mr So and So?' and he said, 'Any pub between here and Woodridge you'll find me.' Next morning, when Catherine was born, it was a very traumatic time. I just, you know, in all the battles and all the things that were going through my mind when I saw her and all the feelings and that, the only thing that I ever really appreciated about it all was that she came into our family, because I know God places them, you know, and I just thought, she's a chance with us. And if she'd been born into his family she had no chance.

In the program Wayne added, 'Seventeen years later I'm pleased she came to us that way, and she's been a wonderful child and I'm pleased she didn't die and we just got on with it. We never looked back again and we just kept going forward and we got through it because we did it together.'

Justin's mental disability and Catherine's physical one has indelibly shaped the Bennetts' family life. I witnessed a stoic acceptance that these children have been given to them and they may not have been exactly what every parent hopes for, but it is their responsibility to look after them. Still, spending so much time with the family I couldn't help thinking about the relentless slog of it all. Trish bore the brunt of it, but Wayne would often have to cut short activities to be home in time for the heavy lifting of bath and bedtime. Wheelchair-bound, Catherine needs full-time care. But she is as sharp as a tack with a delightful sense of humour, and a number of times off camera I saw her pierce her father's serious demeanour with a joke at his expense. And you could sense he loved it.

I think Catherine found it difficult to see herself on television when the story aired. We caught her on the cusp of those difficult adolescent years. When we returned for a follow-up two years later she had lost weight and flowered into the most beautiful young woman. She now works full-time as a receptionist. 'She has a great work ethic,' Wayne brags, 'she never complains. She's got her dad's personality and her mother's charm.'

We saw these qualities in Justin too, and the great love between father and son. Trish remembered something Wayne said just after Justin was born, when a journalist asked if he wanted Justin to be a top-line footballer. Wayne answered, 'No, as long as he's competitive.'

'And he is,' Trish added with tears in her eyes.

Wayne had worked hard to create a culture at the club that was family based. Even the older players looked upon him as a father figure.

We visited the family at their holiday apartment at Caloundra and filmed the riotous occasion of a football match on the beach. There was Justin, head down, slogging through the pack towards a touch-down, as competitive and determined as his father had always been. Roger Carter, our editor, spliced two shots together — Justin scoring on the beach, followed by Bronco great Gordon Tallis scoring a try during the next big match — encompassing both the joy of the moment and the poignancy of what might have been.

During the interview, Wayne talked about how, after losing a big match, coming home to Justin always put things in perspective.

Justin will go for the other team and he's smart enough to realise that he gets up my nose. And he stands out there in the jersey of the opposition and puts his arms out and gives me a big cuddle and then he looks at me and says, 'You're not very happy, are you?' and I say, 'No I'm not' and he says, 'Well, I am because my team won.' So if he wasn't your son and he wasn't disabled you'd just about knock him out. But you can't do that so you give him another cuddle and in the house you go.

And then Wayne really let his guard down and tears came into his eyes as he expressed the desire that Justin might have realised the various achievements Wayne himself had made through the years. 'Because,' he said, 'as I'm proud of him I'd like to think he would be proud of me as well.'

It was a moment so heartfelt that, sitting there before him, I felt the hairs prick at the back of my neck. Tears pooled in my eyes and I knew we were witnessing something uncharted about this most private of men.

Phillipa and I realised we had a very poignant family story, but things were still going awry on the football field. The Broncos suffered a humiliating defeat to the Melbourne Storm, the worst losing margin in the club's history, and the following week lost again to Canterbury, making it five losses in a row.

Wayne recalled that time a few years later at a public forum.

We went through a really tough time and, you know, part of the *Australian Story* is they just about move in with you for that period of time. So it was something that I was trying to deal with — the emotions of getting a football team back on track and then having the ABC team in most of your life. And you know, many days I felt like telling them to go to hell because I needed just one less pressure in my life. But we got through it. I think the worst night, they came to Sydney and we played Canterbury at Telstra Stadium.

I remember it vividly. We got beaten right on full time. We'd lost about four or five in a row. It was a really cruel loss because when you lose right on the full-time hooter it hurts even more. And I remember Vanessa and Phillipa coming down to the dressing room and they didn't want to be there either. They just knew it wasn't going to be a nice night.

A team member grumbled to Phillipa in the dressing room that night that it must have been our crew that was jinxing things. They hadn't started their losing streak until we were filming them. Wayne heard about it and told them to stop blaming others for their own shortcomings. But it was difficult taking the cameras into the dressing room after these matches; we felt like unwelcome visitors at a funeral. You could have cut the disappointment and frustration in the air with a knife.

A few days later we got wind of some dramatic news. Football legend and Broncos captain Allan Langer was to resign. We joined the media throng at the club and witnessed a tearful Langer admit he just didn't have the motivation to play out the rest of the year. It was another blow to Wayne and a club already beaten low.

One of the challenges of documentary-making is that you may have one story in your head, but you have to cope with the reality of what is unfolding before you. It wasn't until we were editing the story that I realised what was happening on the field mirrored the themes of Wayne's life: courage in the face of adversity; hardships faced under pressure. I had no doubt he would turn this around the way he had struggled to turn around so many things in his life.

The last shot of the program was Wayne striding out across an empty stadium and we chose these words to accompany it:

My life has been adversity, but from each disaster I've come back stronger. And even now that we've lost seven games, we're still not the underdogs. I know how to battle through it. I know I'll come out the other side of it and I know they'll come out with me. We'll be stronger people. We'll appreciate winning more than we ever have in the past.

It encapsulated one of Wayne's key messages: that life is not about winning all the time, but about giving your personal best and persevering through the tough times.

When the program went to air, the Broncos needed to win the next ten of the fifteen remaining matches to make it to the final seven that year. Incredibly, they went on to do it, and the next year won the Grand Final again.

The aftermath of the episode surprised me. Feedback came pouring in, stories about how watching a poker-faced public figure let down his guard and expose his emotional flank had made grown men weep. People were surprised to discover that this man of few words thought so deeply about life and his place in it. They couldn't believe the depth of feeling the program showed, exactly what this family had to cope with. A strength of character had been revealed and viewers were moved by it.

The ABC was inundated with requests for a repeat and, over the next few years, obliged too many times for the comfort of Trish, Elizabeth and Catherine, who had felt uncomfortable watching themselves. Justin, however, was very happy with his starring role — so much so that Wayne had to splice together the footage of Justin so he could watch himself wall to wall.

Wayne would say later that it took him thirty years to build his stony-faced, intimidating reputation and thirty minutes for our program to tear it down.

Bennett after yet another Grand Final win for the Broncos.

I tell you what *Australian Story* did, it destroyed a myth. I mean, for thirty years they thought I was cranky and unhappy and everything else. And after thirty minutes, you know, people are ringing up saying he's not such a bad guy. I couldn't believe the turnaround.

But Wayne also knew he had a message to get across, and while he often went to schools to talk to the students, he knew he couldn't get to every school in Australia.

I've got great belief in our young people, you know, and they're totally misunderstood and there's too much criticism of them. They live in a difficult time, but they live in a time where they're very challenged. And so I just wanted to give a message of hope and, hey, you know, doesn't matter how tough you're doing it, you know, you can make something happen, you don't have to keep blaming somebody else. And so through the *Australian Story* that allowed me to do that. The program shows up in schools as part of religious education and education whatever. And so it's been a wonderful vehicle and they've got something out of it. So that's made me happy, you know, that it has made a difference. If it helps some teacher out there that's struggling with a class or a kid or whatever and it makes all the difference somewhere, then it's all been worth it.

I visited the Bennetts again late last year. Elizabeth is now married to footballer Ben Ikin and they have two gorgeous little boys. Catherine was at work that day, Justin was inside watching sport, and it was lovely to talk to Elizabeth and Trish while the boys played on the patio. Our lives had moved on in many ways but still the hard slog of caring for their children day in and day out struck me. I had been on stage with Wayne the night before at an *Australian Story* forum in Brisbane and he'd talked about just that.

Unless you've got children with a disability in your family, you just don't know how tough it is. That story was five years ago and it hasn't got any easier at home, you know, because the demands are there every day. Justin is twenty-seven now and nothing has changed for him, you know, he's full-time care. Catherine's twenty-three and really well adjusted and working. But, you know, she's full-time care and it's just on, it's on every day of our life, and the selfish part of you wants to walk away from it and it would be the easy thing to do. The difficult thing is to stay and to make it work. I know Trish feels the same, you know, you'd just be letting them down, it's not their fault. We wanted children and they didn't turn out the way we wanted them, but that doesn't mean that we can break up our marriage and fall apart because life gets a little difficult.

Wayne Bennett's story is about the heroism of grand feats and achievements on a national stage. But at home he and his family display a quieter heroism: the courage to stay and deal with the difficulties; to find acceptance in the face of the constant and relentless struggle of everyday life.

It was a privilege to share the time we did with Wayne Bennett and his family. My initial response when Phillipa came to me with his story was 'Who's Wayne Bennett?'

Now I regard him as one of my heroes.

The next generation. Left to right: Ben Ikin and Elizabeth, holding Wayne's grandsons; Wayne, Catherine and Trish.

Ivan Milat posing for a family photo, holding a
World War I vintage machine gun at the home
of brother Alex.

Cracking the Milat Code

John Stewart

In 1994, Ivan Milat was arrested and charged with murdering seven young backpackers in the Belanglo State Forest on the outskirts of Sydney.

In 2004, *Australian Story* examined Milat's life over two episodes. John Stewart spent two years researching the program and speaking to members of the Milat family.

Ivan Milat was from a huge family of sixteen. When the news of his arrest came, it hit them like a nuclear bomb. Many of his brothers and sisters were no longer talking to each other; some had changed their names; others had moved interstate. I felt right from the start that the family was the key to answering two questions: what had created Ivan Milat; and was he the only one involved in the appalling crimes?

Much had been written about Ivan Milat and his life, but no one had explained what had made such a vicious killer. For journalists and media commentators, he remained an unfathomable mystery. But the answer was surely there, in the family, waiting to be discovered.

Furthermore, after Milat was found guilty of the seven murders in 1996, the judge suggested it was highly likely there was more than one killer at work in the forest. Many journalists believed the second killer was Ivan's younger brother Richard Milat, but no one from the media had managed to speak to him in over eight years.

After hundreds of phone calls and many face-to-face meetings with the Milats, I felt I was able to piece together some kind of logic to Ivan Milat's life. The family had its secrets, buried deep in the past, and the Milats spoke their own language: one of contraction, lies, denial and loyalty. There were so many different stories it was like walking into a mirror maze. In the end I became lost, but getting lost was the only way to find the truth. I was sure the family had the answers to our questions. The problem was understanding them.

I first saw Ivan Milat in the flesh when I walked into a courtroom in Sydney in 1996. I was working as a reporter for ABC Television news and spent several weeks helping to cover the murder trial.

What struck me about Milat was how ordinary he looked, dressed in a navy cardigan, a white business shirt and tie. Perhaps the only sinister thing about him was his huge arms and shoulders, the bulging muscles. He looked like a guy who could tear your head right off.

Four years later, I started making contact with the Milats and slowly tracked them all down to different parts of Australia. For years they refused to meet me face to face: Ivan always had another appeal — speaking to me could 'compromise him'. Finally, in June 2004, after the High Court rejected Ivan's last appeal, Bill Milat and his wife, Caroline, agreed to meet me. They were the only two people who were still visiting Ivan in gaol.

To get to Bill and Caroline's house I drove down the Hume Highway. Ivan Milat had worked as a labourer building this highway and it was from its roadside that he carefully selected his victims. After about an hour, I had left the city behind. I was struck by how vulnerable I felt, driving into the bush. This was Milat territory; I was about to enter a new world.

Bill and Caroline's house was extremely neat and tidy, with a white picket fence and perfectly mowed lawns. Bill, in his fifties and balding, met me at the front door. When we spoke about Ivan, he raised his hands as if to say, 'What can I do?' I wondered if perhaps Bill realised Ivan was guilty, but couldn't say so in front of his wife.

Caroline was an ardent supporter of Ivan's and convinced he had been framed by the police. She explained to me the various reasons why she believed Ivan was innocent: there was no DNA linking him to the crime scenes; he was never outwardly violent or badly behaved; and the police had planted the backpacks, the victims' clothing and the gun used in the murders in his house.

We'd arranged to visit Ivan inside Australia's highest-security prison, Supermax, at Goulburn in the New South Wales Southern Highlands. Bill drove the four-wheel drive, with me and Caroline in the back. About half an hour into the journey, he turned off the freeway and down a dirt road, not far from the Belanglo State Forest.

It was a bad moment for me. I don't know these people, I thought, and we're not far from the murder scene. What if they were involved?

A few minutes later we emerged from the bush onto a main road leading into Goulburn.

Supermax was ominous and depressing. The unit is housed within another gaol and no one has ever escaped. Inmates are kept in isolation and relocated every few months to stop them becoming familiar with their surroundings. Outside the prison waited a long line of people: single mums with kids; old people with sons doing life.

There was no way the government was going to allow a journalist to meet with their highest-profile inmate, so I waited in the car park while Bill and Caroline went inside. About two hours later they re-emerged, after being sniffed by dogs for drugs and checked by two metal detectors. Their visit with Ivan had taken place inside a metal room, recorded by video cameras.

'How was Ivan?' I asked.

'Good,' Caroline answered. 'He was pretty upbeat today, he's working on another appeal.'

A generous man, Bill had given Ivan $40,000 for his appeals.

The Milats grew up in south-western Sydney on the fringes of the city in a semi-rural area. They were poor. Dad was a Yugoslav migrant who worked as a manual labourer twelve hours a day and returned home late at night. Mum was flat out washing clothes and cooking meals for twelve kids. They were Catholics and Mrs Milat didn't believe in contraception. Her oldest daughters often asked her, 'Mum, why are you having more kids? Aren't there enough of us already?'

By the time the older boys were teenagers, they were running wild and getting into trouble with the police for petty crimes. Most journalists had assumed that if there was any abuse in the family, the parents were somehow to blame. Mr Milat was tough, and a little paranoid after escaping from a communist country. I had a sense, though, that the real conflicts in the family were between the brothers themselves — nine boys living in an isolated hamlet. I had read research that showed psychopaths tend to come from large families of boys, rather than large families of girls, because violence and physical abuse between brothers is far more common.

But it seemed the Milat men had an incredible sense of loyalty to each other. It was them against the world in the early days — and fifty years later, it was still the same. Nevertheless, ten years after Ivan's arrest, cracks were beginning to emerge.

I felt Caroline was deep in denial. I wondered if the real reason she couldn't believe Ivan was a serial killer was because he had babysat her children when they were young. Perhaps she just couldn't accept the thought that she had put her children at risk? Was it too confronting? But if it was, she had paid a high price: she was unable to leave home by herself and often suffered panic attacks.

Ivan and his younger brother Richard enjoy some karaoke.

I believed subconsciously Caroline knew Ivan had killed those people. It was possible that the realisation was buried deep down, but it threatened to break through, like a living nightmare scratching at the edge of her mind.

Bill was the straightest of the boys. He'd held the same job for over thirty years and was a good father. I felt he knew more than he was willing to say about Ivan.

When I asked Bill if Ivan did it, he said, 'No, but anyone who does that deserves the death penalty. They'd get no sympathy from me.' He explained that the police just didn't have the evidence to convict Ivan: 'They had no DNA.'

It was a claim I heard again and again from the various brothers and sisters. By now I had learned the first rule in the Milat family code: never tell on your brother, no matter what he's done. As Bill said, 'In our family we all mind our own business; we don't go interfering in our brothers' and sisters' lives.'

The Milats all knew that Ivan had raped women and had done other 'bad things', but that was his business, not theirs.

Privately, the Milat boys referred to Ivan as The Psycho and told each other, 'Never walk with your back to him'. Some of them had even admitted, 'If Ivan did do it, he was in the right place.'

Ivan had had affairs with four of his brothers' wives. Two of his brothers had threatened to shoot him, but the family's master manipulator had slipped through their fingers. He built himself a reputation for doing 'good deeds' and looking after their mother and their disabled brother, David. Ivan was the first to come around and help out if anything needed doing: mowing lawns, building a new driveway. It was as if he made up for his sexual adventures by acting like a boy scout.

Bill and Caroline were reluctant to put me in touch with anyone else in the family. After several months, I finally found the phone number for Ivan's oldest brother, Alex, who had moved to Queensland shortly before Ivan's arrest in 1994.

To me, Alex was by far the most mysterious of the Milat family. He spoke in riddles and I had a sense that he knew far more than he was willing to say. After many conversations on the phone, he finally told me, 'Ivan would enjoy raping a man as much as a woman. He was just different, some people are like that.'

I couldn't figure it out. The Milat siblings knew that Ivan was crazy and that he had raped people before. They knew his house was full of the backpackers' gear, but they still seemed to believe he was innocent. After speaking to nine of the surviving brothers and sisters, I was confused by the mixed messages — the hints that they knew he was guilty and the absolute denial that he was a serial killer.

I flew up to Queensland to meet Alex. He was fatter than the other brothers and spoke with huge hand gestures. His stories went off on huge tangents, and he would never answer a question about Ivan. He sat back like a big Buddha on the lino floor, his feet stretched out in front of him.

I was intrigued by Alex. He had given a bizarre statement to the police, which had drawn the focus of the biggest police investigation in Australian history onto the Milat family.

Alex had been a member of the Bowral Pistol Club, which was based near the crime scene in the Belanglo State Forest. After the bodies had been discovered, and the media hysteria had reach full crescendo, Alex was heard talking about the murders at the gun club. He had too much to say, too many theories. A local policewoman, also a member of the club, reported him to the murder investigators.

Suddenly Alex was in the spotlight, being forced to make a statement. He had to come up with something. He told police he had seen a car full of men carrying guns, with two girls in the back seat, bound and gagged. The problem was there was far too much detail. He even described the colour of the driver's eyes: a 'tall man with red hair and tattoos on his knuckles'. The police knew it was bullshit, but the statement brought the Milats under the microscope.

I asked Alex about the statement and he still stuck by it. He couldn't admit that Ivan had committed the crimes. Ivan had lived with Alex for a few years when Ivan was single, and Alex had taught him how to shoot. 'Ivan couldn't shoot for shit before I showed him how.'

Later that day, Alex took me and fellow producer, Ben Cheshire, down into his cellar where he showed us five huge handguns, .44 Magnums, and about seven rifles. All were legally licensed. He showed us his bullet-making machine and hundreds of home-made lumps of lead in a big bucket. He'd been having some trouble from a local policewoman, who was reluctant to renew his gun licences. 'I should have throttled the bitch while I still had the strength,' he said. It was a joke, but it said a lot.

After spending several hours with Alex, I asked, 'How old was the guy driving the car full of guys and girls you saw in the forest?'

'He was forty-four,' he answered. The same age as Ivan, when he was committing the murders.

The first part of the Milat code was 'Mind your own business and never tell on your brother'. But there was another important rule, which I discovered by accident while sitting in a café with Bill and Caroline on another visit to the Supermax gaol.

Bill told me how he'd once got a fine for driving through a red light — the camera had caught him. The notice came in the mail and he took it to court and beat the police because the red-light camera had the time wrong. It was a great victory.

I could tell it was a story he'd told many times before and at the end I couldn't help asking, 'But did you do it, Bill? Did you go through the red light?'

Bill's response was, 'Eh, whatever — the time on the camera was wrong.'

The point wasn't whether you had done something wrong or not; the point was whether the police had the evidence to get you for it. It was all about the evidence. Suddenly another piece fell into place; another step in cracking the Milat code.

Was Ivan guilty? He wasn't caught red-handed; there were no witnesses; 'they didn't have any DNA'. The Milats might know he'd done it, but that wasn't point. The evidence was all circumstantial.

And when I thought about it, this belief that life was about the evidence rather than the truth made sense. I'd been told that when the Milat kids were growing up in the 1950s, most of the cops they knew were corrupt. The boys used to sell their stolen cars to Parramatta police. Why should they have any respect for the law with that kind of experience? As far as they were concerned, all police were crooks and would frame you if they could. It was always about the evidence and not whether you had actually committed the crime.

It was a perspective Ivan himself expressed to me many times in a number of letters written from inside Supermax. They were full of reasons why he was innocent, details of legal technicalities and 'mistakes' that had been made during his trial. I was struck by how articulate and intelligent he was.

I asked Bill and Caroline to pass on a phone number at the ABC, then spent five months waiting for about four hours a day in a radio recording booth. Finally, when I'd just about given up, Ivan called.

There were a few beeps and then a recorded message said, 'This is the Department of Corrective Services. If you wish to receive this call say yes.' I said yes, then spoke with Ivan for about six minutes.

He sounded like your average family uncle, polite and reasonable. He asked how I was. But there was no empathy for the victims, who he described as 'Ms this and Mr that'. He talked about the 'assailant' in a distant, formal way, as if referring to a person he'd never met. The only emotion he expressed was self-pity.

I later arranged for Caroline to record many telephone conversations with Ivan — with his permission — and he was always the same. Self-pitying and showing no remorse.

From speaking with Ivan directly I felt I had learned one key thing. He was a psychopath in the classic sense of the term. He had no feeling for others and was totally self-centred. His world consisted only of himself and the satisfaction of his own desires.

When I met Ivan's youngest brother, Richard, I was very nervous. This was the man most reporters and some police considered to be the second killer.

Bill and Caroline had arranged morning tea for us at their house. When I arrived and parked my Toyota Corolla, the wind from a passing truck almost tore the car door off. I knew Richard would judge me instantly by the way I shook his hand and whether or not I made direct eye

Ivan Milat at a family property near Wombeyan Caves in the Southern Highlands.

contact. I couldn't afford to stuff this up. He hadn't spoken to a journalist in eight years and any nervousness from me could blow it. I wanted to interview him on television and it was a big ask.

I recognised Richard straightaway. He was wearing a red and blue check shirt and tracksuit pants. His new wife, Rhonda, was with him. She had wild hair and was very quiet. I had brought a cheap sponge cake with me and was embarrassed by its plainness, but Richard gulped it down with his hands. He looked hungry.

The extraordinary thing about Richard was that despite Ivan accusing him during the trial of being the killer, he had remained loyal to his brother and maintained his innocence. Did he think Ivan did it, I asked.

'No, they didn't have any evidence, they didn't have any DNA.'

On a later visit to Richard's house, I asked if he thought one man could have committed the murders on his own. We were standing in his yard, alone, and he said, 'If I point a gun at ya, I'm either going to shoot ya or ya gonna be submissive.'

Of course, it was in Richard's interest for us to believe there was only one person involved in the crime.

In the end, only one Milat, Boris, had the guts to speak out against his brother. Ivan had had an affair with Boris's wife, Marilyn, and the two brothers had been offside ever since. Boris expressed real remorse and sympathy for the victims' families and called for Ivan to come clean about the five or so other murders he was linked to. But in speaking openly and honestly about his brother, he broke the family code and he paid the price for it. Boris received death threats from his sisters, who said, 'If you talk about it, you can't even imagine the things we will do to you.'

Researching and producing the *Australian Story* programs on Ivan Milat and his family brought me closer to resolving those two questions: what created Ivan Milat the serial killer; and was there anyone else involved in the murders?

The answer to the first question was quite simple. Neglect and abuse — both key features in the background of psychopaths according to the research. All the Milat children had been neglected to some extent: there were just too many kids; their father was never around; their mother was too busy. Ivan never bonded with either parent or anyone else. Kids who grow up without limits placed on them, no personal boundaries, are unsocialised. They become free-floating atoms, detached from society.

By the time Ivan was fourteen he was completely self-centred, with no empathy for anyone. The Milats' home life was chaotic and

Boris Milat. The only Milat prepared to speak the truth about Ivan.

stressful. There was violence and abuse between the brothers. Ivan split off into a fantasy world and often described himself as a cowboy or 'The Saint', from the popular 1960s' television series. He was an intensely private and secretive person. But Ivan was also a narcissist, his ego was also a big part of why he became a serial killer.

Ivan saw himself as a big guy, a success, an all-conquering sexual predator who could have sex with any of his brothers' wives and get away with it. He had a grand self-image. But by the time he was in his forties, his brothers had divorced and their wives had moved away. Ivan's own wife apparently left him after discovering what a nightmare he was to live with. Suddenly Ivan was a middle-aged man living at home with his mother. He was angry and felt like a failure. Police believe he started killing people to build himself up again.

Of course there was more to it. In gaol, Ivan had been raped and had raped other men. He enjoyed sadistic behaviour and got a real thrill out of raping and torturing other people. The murders were his greatest moments; the victims' belongings his private trophies.

One thing that I've learnt from this whole story is that there is very little which separates a rapist from a killer. Ivan Milat was reportedly committing rapes as a teenager, so moving onto killing people was not a big step for him. According to the experts, the act of rape is all about power and having control over other people. Ivan was a rapist who evolved into a sadistic killer, but it was the rapist who was at the core of his personality. He was a rapist and a sadist before he reached his eighteenth birthday; he was a time bomb waiting to go off. Some people are destined to wreak havoc on society and he was one of them. In the end, how much damage someone like Ivan Milat can do in a lifetime probably just comes down to how long they spend out of gaol.

As for the second question was Ivan the only one involved in the murders? To be honest, I still don't have an opinion. Would Ivan have trusted anyone else to be involved? Maybe, but he was a loner and only trusted himself.

There is one certain thing. The first backpackers to be killed in the Belanglo State Forest — Australians Deborah Everist and James Gibson — were not Milat's first victims. The police may be divided about whether there were one or two killers, but no one believes these murders were where Ivan started. There are at least three other victims linked to Milat: all were found in the same area; all were killed in the period leading up to the Belanglo murders.

Based on everything I've learned about serial killers, it's highly unlikely that Milat started out with a couple. Police estimate that Milat has killed somewhere between ten and fifteen people. He began with lone travellers, then, as his confidence grew, worked his way up to couples. If another brother was involved, it's likely Ivan brought him in later, to go for a pair.

Ivan got a big shock when the English tourist, Paul Onions, escaped from his car. He may have got some backup then as well, after Onions got away from him just outside the forest, but only Milat and whoever else was involved knows the answer to that.

I spent three days with the prime suspect, Richard Milat, and I'd like to think he is not the second killer.

Perhaps we will never get to the real truth, not when the majority of the Milats maintain their code of loyalty and silence. They must know that Ivan committed those terrible, sadistic murders, but only Boris was prepared to speak out on *Australian Story*.

When I first started talking to the Milats, I assumed that any family secrets were shared by all the siblings. But over time, I discovered there was one important group of three or four brothers, a kind of little secret society, who knew things the others

Press awaiting the arrival of Ivan Milat as he returns to court in Sydney for the verdict in his trial for the murder of seven backpackers.

didn't. And there's one particular secret they'd kept to themselves — until now.

One day, one of the brothers wanted a camera to take some photos of his newborn baby. He asked around the family and Ivan offered him one with film already in it. The brother took the photos and got them developed. Along with his baby photos were some pictures of two girls he had never seen before. They were young and looked like they were on some kind of holiday. The brother knew Ivan had a lot of women, and thought he must have got lucky.

The brother put the photos in a drawer and forgot about them. A few months later, he was watching the television news and photographs of victims from the Belanglo State Forest murders came up onscreen. They looked vaguely familiar. He went to the drawer, got the photos out and almost had a heart attack. The two girls in the photos were the murdered British backpackers Caroline Clarke and Joanne Walters.

The brother called Ivan on the phone, and Ivan said he'd found the camera by the side of the road and had no idea who the girls were.

His brother was close to a nervous breakdown. The cabal of four brothers had a meeting and decided to burn the photos. At this point, in 1993, one year before Ivan's arrest, they knew for certain that Ivan was the serial killer.

Later, when the police arrested Ivan, they found a camera at his house that was the same make and model as the one owned by Caroline Clarke. They couldn't prove it was her camera, but it was the right type. Ivan had kept Caroline Clarke's camera and forgotten to remove the film.

I was shocked to discover that members of his family knew Ivan was guilty way before his arrest. The photographs were damning evidence, which never made it to court. 'Never tell on your brother; mind your own business; it's all about the evidence.'

The Milat family code swallowed up those crucial photographs.

Dr Michael Holt of Royal Brisbane Hospital, on the beach with his family.

A Life Dissected

Dr Michael Holt

Director of Orthopedics, Dr Michael Holt had it all:
perfect family, perfect house, perfect career. Then came
a terrible fall from grace — a car accident that left him
with dreadful injuries that threatened to destroy his
career and his life.

In 2004 *Australian Story* recounted Dr Holt's
downfall and his courageous fight back to the top.

Here he tells of his experiences in front of
the camera.

I love autobiographies and biographies, stories about people and their lives — I read them all time. It's the human interest element that fascinates me, the complexity of people. After my accident and recovery, I'd given talks at schools, universities and to professional organisations — even the Guide Dogs for the Blind Association — so I knew people found something to identify with in my own story. Nevertheless, I was still surprised when *Australian Story* approached me about doing a program.

In the show, my wife, Julie, described her life before the accident as that of a princess. She had a perfect husband, perfect children, a perfect house, perfect everything. For myself, I'd been lucky enough to grow up in a very loving and supportive family environment and, as an adult, I'd achieved my dream of becoming a doctor. In 1993, I was appointed director of orthopaedics at Royal Brisbane Hospital, and six years later I made the transition into private practice. I suppose you could say I was at the pinnacle of my career. And then, one day, everything changed.

I'd been at the Royal Brisbane doing my all-day surgery. I was crossing the road to go to the bank and suddenly I found myself in front of a car. In a split second, I had to react. I dived over the bumper bar, as I didn't want to be hit in the legs, and apparently I bounced off the windscreen and hit the traffic island. My head and face took most of the impact.

I was very lucky that a bystander had enough sense to turn me on my side. I was lying on my back, choking on my own blood, and sixty seconds later I'd have been dead. Someone else applied pressure with their hand on my neck to slow down the blood loss.

I was taken by ambulance to Royal Brisbane Hospital. By the time I arrived there, I was unrecognisable due to facial fractures and swelling. The initial surgery was to control the blood loss and repair the lacerations through my neck and face. I had what's called a closed head injury or traumatic brain injury. I was unconscious and ventilated for some days, then became aware but not alert.

My first conscious aim was: could I have my life back? Could I ever be what I was before?

As time went on, I realised I couldn't see too well in my right eye. I asked my eye surgeon about it and he said, 'It's buggered.'

'Is there any chance of recovery?' I asked.

'No,' he said, and at that point I knew my life as a surgeon was over. That was devastating and I cried like a baby.

After eight weeks in hospital, I went home. I had a spinal fracture, a paralysed vocal cord, a half-paralysed face. I was deaf in one ear and blind in one eye. I was as weak as a kitten and could hardly stand up because of lack of balance. At that time, I also lost my father. He died in hospital, with his ten children at his bedside.

When I got home from hospital, life was pretty awful. I felt that my perfect life had been utterly destroyed. When I woke up in the morning, my day was black. When I went to bed at night it was still black, and it had been black all day. There was no respite. Depression is a terrible thing. It's a scourge on society.

The only positive thing I could see was that we had been insured. If we hadn't been, we would have lost the house, the car — we'd have had to sell everything just to survive. My marriage may have failed too. I would have had to deal with all that as well as rehabilitating. I could never have survived that.

During my rehabilitation it helped to have specific things to focus on. I had to set myself goals. At first I started off just throwing a football in the backyard with the kids. And I built things around the house — my family called me Bob the Builder.

Charlie Earp, Greg Norman's coach, called me one day to see how I was going. I told him I didn't think I'd ever play golf again, not with losing the sight in one eye, and he said, 'Oh, no worries. I know lots of guys with one eye. I've got Australian amateur champions with one eye.' So he got me back into golf and, with Charlie's help, I even ended up improving on the handicap I'd had before the accident.

I also took part in the Noosa triathlon six months after being released from hospital, and I trained very hard for that. So those achievements helped me and I thought: what's the next step here? Of course, it was work.

After two years at home in rehabilitation, I wanted my life back. I wanted to return to my private practice, to what I had before. Just before I went back to work, though, the Medical Board received an anonymous phone call from a GP who said, 'Holt's half deaf, half blind, and he's going back to work. Look into it.'

I approached Royal Brisbane, the teaching institution and my old hospital, and asked them to assess and supervise me. I was prepared to change profession if they found I could no longer do my job properly.

For the first month, I was allowed to be an intern and nothing more. I was allowed to assist at very simple surgery and had to report all my consultations to a senior doctor. That was difficult because I'd been director at the hospital before the accident. I'd taught and supervised some of the men who were now my supervisors.

I think the turning point for me was operating on Bruce Randall. I'd known Mr Randall for almost eight years: he'd suffered multiple car accidents and his doctor in Hobart had recommended amputating both legs and his arm. I'd mapped out a surgical strategy instead: I'd do his left arm, his right wrist and then his knees. I had achieved part of that when I stopped work because of my own accident, so it was marvellous to be able to pick up where I'd left off.

It was one of the best operations I'd ever done. And afterwards I thought, well, where's the impaired doctor here? There is no impaired doctor here. I was doing what I had always done.

After that the hospital employed me as a staff surgeon. I should have been happy: I was alive, fit, my golf handicap was low, I was working again as a surgeon. But it wasn't enough. I wanted my full licence restored so I could return to private practice. And around that time, the Medical Board — who were running an ongoing impairment investigation — contacted me again and said, 'We want you to agree not to go into private practice until we have tested you further.' The shock was like a bolt of lightning. We'd achieved so much and now it looked as though it could all go sour.

It took another nine months to satisfy the Medical Board that there was no impairment. When the decision came, it was a huge weight lifting off my shoulders. I can't describe the sense of elation. It was only at that point that I felt I had finally recovered.

Australian Story producer Claire Forster approached me after a talk I gave at the Gabba. 'That's a terrific story,' she said. 'We'd like to film it — would you tell it for us?'

I wasn't intimately familiar with *Australian Story* or its style and so Claire gave me a couple of previous episodes to look at. One of them was the Wayne Bennett piece, which is a very powerful story, and I thought it was just marvellous. Wayne is an idol of mine anyway, so the fact that he'd trusted the ABC to that extent had a big influence on my decision. I could see that *Australian Story* was a genuine program about genuine people. However, it was still a leap of faith!

The other thing was, I liked Claire right from that first meeting. She was very honest about the filming, saying, 'It's a complicated process. It's time-consuming and you may find it intrusive, so I want you to be aware of all that.'

We also discussed some personal issues that I didn't want covered in the program. 'I won't be talking about this on television,' I said.

Claire was fine with that. 'People talk to us differently on *Australian Story*,' she said. 'People trust us, and I think there's a reason for that.'

Right from the beginning, that important issue of trust was out in the open and I felt very comfortable because of that.

I didn't actually find the filming intrusive — and I don't think my wife or children did either — but it was very time-consuming. They filmed me at home, at work, in lots of different locations. I remember Anthony, the cameraman, telling me early on in the process, 'Listen, pal, this won't be finished until it airs,' and he was right.

The main interview took place at our home. The crew came and set up in front of a window, with a vase of flowers in the background — I think that must be an *Australian Story* thing because I've noticed it on other programs. Claire was very clever in how she conducted the interview. The way it appears on the show, the interviewer isn't present — it's just the person whose story it is talking to the camera.

Claire had heard me speak at various events, so she asked me questions that fed into that, so I was effectively telling my story in a familiar way. Of course, there were some things we covered in greater depth, and topics that I don't usually touch on during my public talks, but overall I felt the process worked well. When I saw the final result, I was extremely impressed with how they wove the interview into the other footage.

Part of the program was a re-enactment of the accident. They filmed it at the actual site and, coincidentally, it was exactly the same time of day. I've been past the spot many times, on my bike, in the car, but I'm not one to dwell on things. My attitude is, well, you've got to get on with your life, so I chose not to be affected by it every time I passed by.

When we got there to film the re-enactment, I wouldn't say I was spooked, but I was aware of the traffic going by and the fact that this was where I'd stepped out and it had all happened.

The cameraman, Anthony, was very clever. I could see him working out the angles to shoot from, how it would look when it was edited. They used a dummy and threw it at a car, then smashed the car windscreen with a hammer, so it ended up being fairly graphic.

My wife and I accepted that we'd have no editorial control over the program, but we were a bit worried about how the children would respond to the re-enactment. Claire allowed me to see that footage beforehand, just to reassure me, and I thought it was fine. The children know what happened, they know it was serious, and I didn't think it would affect them any more than watching other programs on television.

It was all a question of trust really, and I was confident the ABC would do the right thing. When they were checking their facts for information they wanted to use at the end of the program, for example, they said, 'We'd like to say that Dr Holt has done well, but he could go blind in his other eye at any moment.'

There is a very remote chance of that, and it made for a dramatic ending, but I didn't want the last enduring image to be the idea that I could go blind at any time. I was thinking of my patients — imagine going into a knee operation and worrying that your surgeon might go blind in the middle of it! So I asked if it would be possible to find an alternative ending and when I had explained my concerns, they agreed.

I was a bit apprehensive on the night of the broadcast. I don't really like to see myself on television. I tended to focus on the injuries and the paralysis. That sense of, oh God, did I really look like that?

My mother and brother came over to watch the program with us, and my neighbours, who have been very good friends through all this. Their son, who was just seventeen at the time of the accident and had only had his licence for a week, drove my wife to hospital when she got the call to say I was injured.

So we all watched it together and, overall, we were very pleased with the outcome. The team did a beautiful job with all the material they had, and even though I knew the whole story and every inch of the footage, I still shed a tear watching it put together in that way. Julie and my mother were in tears too; it really was a very moving occasion.

I did have one minor criticism. There was a piece of footage I'd seen of the President of the Medical Board saying, 'We have tested that man for a long time. We can find nothing wrong with him'. I thought that was going to be in the show but it wasn't, and I was disappointed about that because I feel that some in the medical profession believe that I got some kind of special dispensation from the Medical Board. They say to me, 'Gee, you're going great, but are you actually operating as a surgeon?' They don't quite accept that I've been judged perfectly fit and capable of continuing in my profession. So it would have been nice to have the Medical Board President proclaiming that publicly.

I was also rather surprised by the impression created in the show that I was universally disliked in the hospital before the accident. I had people ringing me up afterwards, saying, 'What was that about? We didn't see you like that.' It's true that when you are director of a public institution, you can't be everyone's friend, but some of the people who made those comments on the show felt that what they said had been over-emphasised.

The implication was that I was a horrible person before the accident and now I'm a nice guy. It's certainly true that I deal with people differently now, so I can understand that impression in some part, but the accident didn't change who I am as a person. It just made a difference to how I approach life, perhaps.

The public reaction to the program was quite extraordinary. I knew that *Australian Story* was a popular program, but I wasn't expecting anything like the response that came. Lots of people contacted me or contacted the ABC. One fellow, a friend I played rugby with fifteen years before, wrote and said, 'Good on you, Holtie, I knew you had it in you'.

When you have that kind of accident, many people don't really know what happened and they're afraid to just ring up and ask how you're feeling; they don't want to interfere. The thing is, of course, when you're sick that's exactly when you want people to get in touch. So it was nice that people were able to see how it had all worked out.

Some people have asked, 'Michael, are you a better doctor as a consequence of what's happened to you?'

They like to think that I have embraced my misfortune and become a better person because of it. But the accident wasn't some kind of stepping stone for me. I'm the same doctor now as I was before, with the same skill. Actually, I do think I'm probably a little better than I used to be, because of my change in attitude. But the accident itself didn't make me a good person; I was a good person before.

My truthful response is: I wish it had never happened. I can't blink; I can't blow out candles; I can't wolf-whistle at my wife. I have permanent reminders every day that I'm impaired. And every day I wake up with the knowledge that I could go completely blind. Each morning I think, I hope it's not today. It sounds melodramatic, but that's the reality of the situation.

That said, I have gained things from the experience. I'm probably a calmer person now, a bit more reconciled, not as driven. And I appreciate the extra time I've had to spend with my family.

When I got the letter from the Medical Board giving me permission to return to private practice, I said, 'Righto, kids — we're gonna throw my work boots in the bin. Bob the Builder has retired.'

My youngest son was very upset. He said, 'Dad, I don't want you to retire Bob the Builder. I like Bob the Builder! I like him at home, I like him doing things.'

And he went and got the work boots out of the bin and put them in his own wardrobe.

That made me much more conscious about keeping hold of the things I'd gained through the accident. Now, when the boys come out in the morning in their dressing-gowns, all warm and toasty from bed, I think, oh God, I'm glad I didn't miss that. I wake up now and think, God I'm lucky to have what I have. We are a very fortunate family.

Simon Illingworth, shortly after he rejected a $250,000 offer from Victoria Police.
Had he accepted the money, he would no longer have been able to 'speak ill' of the force.

One Man Standing

Belinda Hawkins

In 2004, Melbourne seemed to be overwhelmed by a gangland war that relied in part for its survival on police corruption.

At the height of the media coverage of this crisis *Australian Story* broadcast an exclusive account of a senior detective in internal affairs who blew the whistle on that corruption.

Detective Sergeant Illingworth's compelling story prompted an unprecedented public response and pushed further the argument for a Royal Commission into the troubled Victoria Police.

Simon Illingworth is built like a tank. Watch him on the footy field, where he plays full forward for his old private school, and you'll see he's no pushover. He runs at players, hip and shoulders them to one side. If you were casting a police officer in a TV show, he'd be perfect: beefy, blond and confident. But looks can be deceiving, and that's what made Simon's Illingworth's story so compelling.

In early 2004, there were reports of people in Melbourne being shot down in broad daylight. It was a gangland war gone nuts; Melbourne felt like a city under siege. I'd heard of a police officer called Simon Illingworth, who was involved in investigating corruption within Victoria Police, but when we first contacted him it seemed all he wanted to talk about was a venture he was setting up outside of his day job, teaching ethics to a wide range of groups. And if that was all he was about, we weren't interested.

Our first meeting took place at the house of a friend of Simon's, where he was camping out. Even though I wasn't sure if we had a story, I knew enough about the dangers to those involved in police internal affairs investigations to feel very nervous going over there. After a series of execution-style killings, Melbourne had become a paranoid place. I was too scared to drive my own car there. What if the house was under surveillance by an underworld killer or bent cop? I didn't want those kinds of people knowing my number plate.

We sat at the kitchen table and Simon stumbled through an account of what was happening to him in Victoria Police. I was transfixed. This was a man who had been commended for his work in bringing successful prosecutions against corrupt officers. But he'd also been bashed, isolated and threatened — not by crooks, but by other police officers.

'I can't believe I'm telling this to a journalist,' he muttered at one point.

For my part, I could barely believe my ears. This is all just too bizarre to be true, I thought.

As a journalist, my job involves parachuting into situations I often know very little about. A sixth sense is vital to work out the lie of the land. In *Australian Story* that sixth sense is even more important, as we have to work out what makes a person tick, as well as what is going on and where the truth lies. I wasn't convinced yet that we had a story in Simon Illingworth — I would wait to see what another meeting brought.

The next time I saw Simon we were filming him surfing at his favourite spot on the Victorian coast, not far from the Twelve Apostles. It was late in the day. One minute he was out there in the spray and the choppy waves, a rip pushing him ever closer to treacherous rocks; the next minute he'd disappeared from the viewfinder. The cameraman was stumped. For a second I was horrified — I wondered if Simon had decided enough was enough and checked out of life. Far from it. He came back into vision, single-mindedly hunting down a wave. This must be how he does his job too, I thought. Goes at it head-on.

In a nearby coffee shop later that morning, the front page of the *Herald-Sun* was everywhere. The main headline was: Action taken on bent cops, new powers due in war on corruption. As Simon read the piece, his mouth started to quiver.

I asked what it was about the article that was affecting him. His eyes filled with tears. 'Here we go,' he muttered and his face crumpled.

I knew then that his was a story worth telling — not because I was taken aback watching his strong face fall apart, rather because whatever caused that kind of hurt needed to be exposed. This guy's for serious, I thought; this is what working as a cop has done to him. The job Simon loved was killing him. It might be too late for him, but he wanted the pain to stop for others. He wanted to be proud of Victoria Police once again.

Simon turned away from me and the camera stopped rolling. I watched him walk over to the water and thought, that's it, now he's shown his heart he'll pull out of the project. Just as I'm thinking there's a story here. Before we've even started on the actual interview.

Simon came back to finish his coffee and cigarette, then we got into the car and headed back to Melbourne.

'Are you going to go through with this?' I asked, finally.

He turned to me, astonished. 'I'm not backing out if that's what you're worried about,' he said. 'Someone's got to do it.'

Detective Sergeant Simon Illingworth was the first serving member of Victoria Police ever to speak out about problems in the force. A number of high-profile current affairs programs had got wind of his experiences and tried to woo him, but Simon didn't want to be seen as slagging off colleagues in a 'good cop/bad cop' story. He didn't want the whole thing to be sensationalised, and he wasn't looking for payment. He'd lost confidence in the reporters he saw around the courts, but it still took him a long time to decide to talk to *Australian Story*. He didn't have clearance from Victoria Police to do so. He just did it. He decided he had no option.

At the age of nineteen, Simon was studying economics at university but spent far too much time surfing with his mates. His mother was starting to think he'd never amount to anything. But then she took him to the police academy open day. When Simon saw all the wild and wonderful 'save the world' things a police officer could do, he signed up. Victoria Police promised a life of endless adventure.

In his graduation video, you see a young man marching confidently, clearly proud to be wearing that uniform. After all, Victoria Police was thought to be the greatest force in the country. It had a long and noble tradition of being squeaky clean. It took just two years for Simon to experience first-hand how far from the truth that was.

By 1989 Simon was working as a constable at Melbourne's City West station. A new sergeant arrived with a big reputation. The Sergeant came from the Armed Robbery Squad,

Victoria's Police Chief Commissioner Neil Comrie and Constable Simon Illingworth on his graduation day.

where the big men made their names. He hand-picked his crew and Simon Illingworth was one of them.

'We thought, this guy's a legend,' Simon told us during his *Australian Story* interview. 'He was what I wanted to be. I wanted to become, you know, a gun detective.'

But young Constable Illingworth found himself drawn into a compromising situation when he saw the Sergeant pocket cash from a raid on an illegal gambling venue. Simon didn't speak out and, seeing that the young officer knew how to turn a blind eye, the Sergeant took matters further. A lot further. He tried to get Simon involved in a bizarre plot to kidnap a drug dealer called Ray Baxter.

Simon got the clear impression that the Sergeant wanted to take Baxter out to a tip and do away with him. Why? He still doesn't know. Simon was well aware of who Baxter was: he'd had to rugby tackle him while booking him for drug offences. He was in a bind. He knew that what the Sergeant was asking him to do was very wrong. He also knew that to dob on your superior was a crime against a long-standing if unspoken police code of behaviour.

In the end, Simon went to Internal Affairs.

The Sergeant pleaded guilty and was sentenced to four years jail. Meanwhile, Simon Illingworth's life in the force went from bad to worse. He was marked out as some kind of mad rookie. Worse, a whistleblower. Filth.

The Sergeant had lots of powerful police mates: one threatened to kill Simon as he went into court to give evidence against the Sergeant. A former officer king-hit Simon from behind as he was having a drink after work. He was passed up for promotion time and time again.

When Simon was telling us his story, he often spoke in riddles and half sentences. In researching the program, I came across a lot of people who talked about police stories like that, journalists included. There's a lot of code language and cops-and-robbers jargon that is gobbledegook to someone not experienced in crime reporting. It made it difficult to get a strong sense of what was beneath the riddles. I wondered if, in fact, Simon was just a very paranoid individual. In the bigger scheme of things, did any of his story so far really matter to anyone not fixated by the idea of Melbourne as a city run by drug dealers and crooked cops?

Then I started reading the court transcripts of the officer who threatened to kill Simon at court. I still didn't get it. In 1990, Supreme Court Justice Ken Marks wrote: 'There is nothing ... to suggest that Illingworth ... concocted or imagined the events of which he complained ... He appeared perfectly normal in the witness box, albeit at an early age caught up in the cross-currents of factional strife and morality standards in the police force.'

I went out looking for police who had worked with Simon during those early years. Off the record I started to get a picture of an officer who was popular with others. Colleagues respected him because he had a knack for catching crooks, because he was good at football, because he liked a beer and girls liked him. One former colleague — let's call him Bill — left Victoria Police some years ago, sick of its culture, but kept up his friendship with Simon.

'Simon is someone everyone has an opinion of,' he told me. 'He had to work twice as hard because of the white-anting that went on around him after he went to Internal Affairs. Unless you're in the club, you're nobody.'

Simon's problem was that he was becoming a 'somebody' — somebody others didn't want around any more.

In 2002 Bill and his father met up with Simon for a Christmas drink at the Celtic Club Hotel in Melbourne. By that time Simon had moved to the Ethical Standards Department and his job was to investigate crooked cops. It was the best and worst place for someone with his history. Bill turned from the bar and saw Simon's face was ashen. A suspended cop he was investigating had just walked past him with a well-known underworld crime figure. The mobster stopped and glared at Simon menacingly. Bill took his mate outside and asked him if he was all right. Stupid question. He wasn't. Simon was shaking and couldn't speak. Bill watched him walk away.

Bill hadn't seen the incident take place, but the hotel's video camera did. The heads are blurry but unmistakable. Simon could see no reason for the two men to be in that pub that night other than to intimidate him.

I desperately wanted to use Simon's copy of the video footage. Here was evidence of police involvement in underworld crime: a suspended detective out with a violent crim, seemingly out to intimidate the very officer who was investigating them. The officer was off duty, out with mates. All this contradicted the state government's and Police Commissioner's line that there was no connection between police and gangland criminals.

Simon flatly refused. He was already pushing the boundaries just in talking to us. To release evidence like that would be over-stepping the mark. It could interfere with court proceedings. He had charged the police officer on the tape and the case was still to be heard. Simon's desire to see due process followed overrode his desire to make a point. But he talked about it on camera: the secret was out.

The world of police internal affairs, otherwise known as the Ethical Standards Department, sounds like a murky, unhappy place. Simon wasn't the only officer likely to be under stress; there were at least two others. One had found police-issue bullets in his letterbox at home. Another's wife was followed by a suspect as she took their child to kindergarten. But I couldn't find anyone else willing to go public with a first-hand account of what it was like — until I met former Detective Superintendent Neil O'Sullivan.

Neil O'Sullivan is what's known as an old-style cop. He's rotund and tough and swears like a trooper. I watched Simon squirm as Neil told me a string of over-the-top and often lewd stories, but I've seldom laughed so much during an off-the-record discussion. Neil was Simon's boss and he's something of an unsung hero. He has a Google-like capacity to recall details on just about anything you ever wanted to know about Victorian crime. Neil was trying to clean up Victoria Police and set up a unit inside Internal Affairs designed to catch out officers who looked like they might take up with crims before they got into it too far. The idea was to be proactive rather than simply punitive. Both Simon and Neil were devastated when the force broke up the unit in 2002. Devastated and disillusioned.

Neil was also Simon's mentor and reeks of ethics and integrity. When Neil went on camera and talked openly about how Victoria Police betrayed Simon, as well as about wider problems in the force, our story really came together. I got a sense of the way in which the force was letting down an awful lot of honest cops and, in doing so, was also letting down the community it purported to serve.

Once the interview shoots were over, my big concern was keeping it all under wraps. I started to write the story, but I was worried Simon might not last the distance. He knew he couldn't see anything of the script or the edit before the story went to air; he just had to wait and go on trusting me. I knew what that was doing to him, but my responsibility was to get his story out, to make sure it was factually accurate and fair. Yet this was no clinical summary of a police officer's career. Simon and Neil had bared their souls and I could not help but feel responsible for their well-being.

A former colleague rang to help out with background. She'd heard we were doing something on police corruption, but I couldn't tell her what. She knew a Simon Illingworth was off on stress leave. She knew the cop he'd arrested and feared. I listened to her talk, but I couldn't tell her anything. I felt dreadful, but I had no choice. I'd promised Simon and Neil that, until the story went to air, I would keep secret the fact that they were breaking ranks.

It's difficult to prepare someone for what's in store when they agree to tell their story on *Australian Story*. I have yet to meet someone who regrets it; but I've also yet to meet someone who doesn't feel utterly washed out by the process at various stages of the shoot.

Telling the story means reliving the trauma. It means breaking through the barrier of 'I'm okay now' that many people throw up around themselves. We need to find out what really happened and what it was really like, which means going over and over parts of the story. Then there's the filming itself — both of the main interviewee and the people around them — as we try to illustrate their story with pictures. This process can be a lot of fun. It can also be extremely draining.

When the program is about someone who is still living the trauma or, at the very least, is still raw from the experience, I worry that the process of reliving events might tip them over the edge altogether. I was sick with worry about what speaking out was doing to Simon Illingworth.

Towards the end of the shoot, cameraman Ron Ekkel and I followed Simon to the house he'd had to sell after his marriage collapsed. He needed to clear out the back shed. No big deal. But as Ron started to film, we could see that all was not as it seemed. Simon went at the boxes with a vengeance, lugging one after another to his trailer. His enormous frame was heaving not with the load, but with the stress of coping with a life gone off the rails. He loved his house. It cut him to pieces to leave.

Ron and I wanted to turn away and leave him be. Simon didn't like being filmed; it made him self-conscious. He felt like an idiot. The camera kept rolling though. And Simon was so trapped in his own world that this time he was oblivious to it. Ron is a super fit, super keen cameraman who has covered some of the bloodiest wars around over the past ten years. Later, Ron and I talked about what we'd seen that day. 'It's quite powerful and tough to feel someone go through all the emotions and to let it out, piece by piece,' Ron said. 'I was there filming Simon's every move and emotion,' Ron continued. 'I apologised to him while doing it and explained I would do so as sympathetically and quickly as possible. It must be so hard to be so alone when you are doing what you know to be right. I admired his guts.'

Getting the story to air was a nightmare. *The Australian* was running an article about the Ethical Standards Department officer who received bullets in the mail. I thought we needed to get Simon's episode up fast. Editors Roger Carter and Angela Trabucco worked around the clock to weave together the pictures and sound we had accumulated over almost one month. The story was rescheduled to broadcast a week earlier than planned. That's a lifetime in television production.

Two nights before the program showed, Simon emailed me saying that if he couldn't get any other job after doing *Australian Story*, at least he could try out as a cocktail shaker. He was sick with nerves.

He wasn't alone. On the night of the broadcast, Neil O'Sullivan went and sat on the back doorstep with his dog. His wife pleaded with him but he wouldn't budge. It was only as the *Australian Story* theme music came on that his family managed to persuade him back inside to watch.

The public response to the story was unprecedented. One woman wrote to Simon's mother saying that he reminded her of the boys she had farewelled as they went off to fight in World War II: honest and courageous; heroes every one of them. She had thought those characteristics had died on the battlefield fifty years ago, but Simon proved that some Australians still held them dear.

Serving members of police forces around Australia and New Zealand wrote in with similar stories, all expressing relief that someone finally had the guts to speak out.

Simon's story also made the news for a long time afterwards. It fuelled debate over whether there should be an independent inquiry into corruption within Victoria Police, if not a royal commission. The opposition raised Simon's story repeatedly in the state parliament. The Police Commissioner took to talkback radio, agreeing that Simon was an outstanding officer but stopping short of addressing the details of his allegations. It was extraordinary to watch.

Ray Baxter's wife rang me. Baxter was the man Simon had once arrested and then helped save when he blew the whistle on the Sergeant's kidnapping plot. I met with Baxter, who said he was now straight and in full-time work. He was overwhelmed at seeing his fate played out on television. He said the last time he saw Simon, the young officer had suggested they have a game of pool one day. He wants to do that now: his shout. A way of saying thanks.

Simon could be up for it too. Maybe catching up with Baxter would help put some demons to rest. After all, it was the incident involving Baxter that marked the end of Simon's innocence and the beginning of the end of his career.

Simon's story isn't over yet. Like many officers in Internal Affairs, fear is his constant companion. And it's contagious.

After the program went to air, I received a series of prank calls at home. They came each time I caught up with Simon and had what I imagine was the desired effect. Once I was so shaken I rang the school to check my children had arrived safely that morning. The receptionist said they hadn't showed up in roll call and promised to look around the yard for them. Ten minutes passed. I thought my life was over. So did the crew I was travelling with at the time. My mobile rang. The children were there. They'd dawdled and missed the bell. They were fine. I was anything but.

Several months later, Simon volunteered to talk at a public high school in Melbourne's rough western suburbs. It was a far cry from the school he'd gone to; these teenagers were seriously underprivileged. But Simon wasn't there as a Pied Piper figure, leading them along the pathway to ethical redemption. No. He was there to tell them it's okay to seek help when you're not coping.

Simon Illingworth and Belinda Hawkins at the Victoria Police Awards.

'Champions aren't always the ones who come first,' he told them. 'I've suffered post-traumatic stress — similar they say to that of the Vietnam vets. I've still got a number of court cases to go. My job, my tour, is not over yet. But it will be one day. I often see a psychologist — not because I'm a loser or nuts, but to help me be the best I can be.'

One fifteen-year-old boy asked Simon why, given he was so into ethical behaviour, did he talk without police permission?

Simon paused for a moment, then explained that he'd had no choice. What was wrong in the police had ripped that element of choice from him.

'Do you regret appearing on *Australian Story?*' asked another teenager.

Simon's response was unequivocal: no.

There have been some changes. That's because what was a grey area, an unspoken area — the code of silence, the brotherhood — has been broken. I put it on the table. People have to debate it, they have no choice. My decision to put myself under the microscope on TV was not one I really wanted to do. I didn't seek some sort of fame or want to have people recognise me. It was sort of personal, because I wanted to free myself of carrying my life's achievements, the things I'd been involved with, around with me. Very few people knew. Whilst I was anonymous, it was continually asking for more intimidation and threats. So to some extent it was personal. I got something out of it.

I was extremely stressed about it though. I knew I had to do the *Australian Story*. I knew it deep down. Not for me, but for the next Simon Illingworth, the next whistleblower. Ultimately I knew my story had to be told, and I knew it was going to stress me out because it meant I had to go through all of my life, all those really ordinary occurrences, and package it all up in twenty-eight minutes of TV. I still have trouble watching it. I haven't watched the whole show, not in one sitting anyway.

I sat on the floor watching and listening. Here were fifty or more teenagers, who looked as if current affairs was the very last thing on their minds, utterly gripped by what Simon was saying. They were asking the very question that had played in my mind since we'd finished the edit: what was it like taking part in our program?

Simon's eyes started watering. He was answering from the heart. He was far from over it.

The questions kept coming. 'Are you scared of walking down the street?'

Simon replied:

No, it's different for me now, every now and then someone will walk up to me and say, 'Aren't you that guy on *Australian Story?*'

I'll think, oh here we go, and say yes. They'll say, 'Mate, that was bloody awesome.' And whilst it's just a really little thing — it just lifts you. It makes it worthwhile that you've got people backing you. You no longer feel like you're isolated, like you're on your own. I'm coming to terms with everything that I've been through, and that's why I'm here. I'm back on track almost. I've just got to get through these court cases.

A voice from the side: 'After what you've put your family through, do you think it's worth it. Would you do it all again?'

Simon's voice catches. 'Yes,' he gets out. 'My girlfriend … these court cases are ongoing so we have this constant stress. She's losing her hair. That's very difficult to justify for me.'

I watched the kids leave after the talk. I hoped they'd got it.

A ten-year-old girl called Eliza did. She used the newspaper coverage of Simon's story in a social studies project.

'I can understand what Simon has been through,' she wrote, 'because in Year Four someone bullied me, picked on me and called me names. It made me feel small. I am not usually like that. I am usually strong and confident. She made me feel weak inside. Other girls who I thought were my friends joined her. They told me that friends don't dob on friends. So I didn't. But I learnt real friends don't bully and real friends just don't stand by and watch.'

If a ten year old can get it, let's hope that, one day, police management does.

Simon Illingworth has since resigned from the police force. In his interview for *Australian Story* he said that all he wanted in life was a white picket fence — not to keep people out, but to keep children in. He's got that now. It's not everything, but it is a start.

Simon Illingworth surfing at the Victorian Coast.

Governor-General Peter Hollingworth speaks to the media outside Yarralumla, after a meeting with Prime Minister John Howard, 21 February 2002.

The Gilded Cage

Helen Grasswill

In February 2002 the then Governor-General of
Australia, Dr Peter Hollingworth, created a national
crisis by comments he made on *Australian Story* about
the sexual abuse of a woman by a priest. These
remarks were a major cause of his eventual resignation
as Governor-General — ending one of the most
controversial episodes in Australia's vice-regal history.

It was one of those beautiful, crisp, clear, sunny Canberra days. Driving through the gilded gates and along the magnificent tree-lined avenue that leads to the sprawling buildings of Yarralumla, I thought for the millionth time how fortunate I was to have such an interesting job. Little did I realise how surreal it was about to become.

My colleague Kristine Taylor had arranged for me to meet the Governor-General, Peter Hollingworth, who at the time, January 2002, was under fire for his handling of sexual abuse allegations during his previous tenure, as Anglican Archbishop of Brisbane.

The trouble had flared up following successful court action against the Brisbane diocese by a young woman who, years earlier as a twelve year old, had been abused repeatedly by a sexually depraved teacher at the church-run Toowoomba Preparatory School.

Kristine, one of our two researchers, had first been assigned to approach Peter Hollingworth immediately after Prime Minister John Howard announced his appointment as Governor-General-Designate in April 2001. Our hope — unfulfilled — was that he might agree to appear on *Australian Story* in the two-month lag before formalisation of his vice-regal position on 29 June. So, when his name became embroiled in media coverage of the Toowoomba Prep scandal in early December that year, Kris was quick off the mark with a renewed written request, which she followed up with numerous phone calls and correspondence.

In normal circumstances, incumbent governors-general do not give media interviews, but Dr Hollingworth's situation had become so precarious — already there were calls for his resignation, and no sign of criticism abating — that he felt he had to do something. *Australian Story*, of course, was not the only contender to tell his tale. This was the hottest story in the country and every media outlet was chasing it. Kristine had ensured that we were among the few permitted to present a request in person, so my task, on 24 January 2002, was to continue her good work and get the Governor-General 'across the line'.

Persuading the Governor-General to choose our program above all other options was a very big ask, primarily because of our strict policy of editorial independence. He would have to agree to a 'spill all' interview with no areas of questioning off limits and also accept that we would have total control over what went to air. On the plus side, however, I felt confident that the Governor-General and his advisers would recognise that we had no political or religious agenda and would give him a fair hearing.

I arrived about half an hour early for this initial meeting and it impressed me that Dr Hollingworth didn't keep me waiting. I was ushered straight in to his large but unimposing office. It was a promising start.

Dr Hollingworth was affable, though clearly under a lot of stress. He didn't have the confident bearing of a powerful man, as one might expect of a Governor-General and former archbishop, but his current situation was so unusual that I decided not to jump to any conclusions about him. He'd asked his wife, Ann, to join us. In contrast to her husband, Ann Hollingworth was feisty and didn't mince her words. She'd had some bad experiences with the media and was understandably wary. Far from unsettling me, Ann's directness was something I warmed to.

Two other people also participated in this meeting, the Governor-General's official secretary, Martin Bonsey, and his media adviser, Claire Tedeschi. I liked them both immediately. They were obviously honest, realistic and — thankfully — devoid of 'spin'.

The discussion was congenial, but not easy. The others did the questioning and I answered frankly, irrespective of whether or not my answers were what I thought they wanted to hear. That's an approach I always take. I heard later that two of our serious competitors for this story had appeared more accommodating, but this was counterproductive and caused some suspicion at Yarralumla, which helped swing the decision our way. Undoubtedly, several other factors were also at play: our long-standing request for an interview; the program's reputation for fairness; and, I daresay, the fact that many other prominent people including Prime Minister Howard and his family had previously appeared on the program and respected it.

Whatever the considerations, when I finally left for the airport five hours later I was pretty certain the story was ours, and confirmation came through the following day.

When I relayed the good news to our executive producer, Deborah Fleming, she was very pleased indeed, and I think perhaps a little surprised — pitching for a story like this was an absolute long shot.

Deb is a quite extraordinary executive producer. She's incredibly supportive of everyone on the team and seems to have an innate knowledge of how far she can push each individual. She'd not put any pressure on me whatsoever prior to my meeting with Dr Hollingworth, but now it was action stations. On average, *Australian Story* programs take two or three months to produce, but due to the newsworthiness of this story we both knew that we needed to get it to air as quickly as possible. After factoring in the Governor-General's availability for filming — Australia Day commitments ruled out the next few days — and allowing time for editing, legal checks and so on, we decided to aim for a ridiculously tight three-week turnaround.

I now had just four days to prepare for what was clearly a major interview and intensive film shoot. As I would be the only journalist to be granted this access to the Governor-General, I felt a responsibility to ensure that the interview was thorough and wide-ranging. I'd already negotiated for a full day to be set aside for the interview alone, and somehow I now had to plough through an enormous amount of research material — books, historical information, legal documents, newspaper clippings, as well as recent and archival news and current affairs stories. I guess adrenalin kicked in and enabled me to manage on just a few hours' sleep each night, and I returned to Canberra knowing I had all bases covered.

Mind you, I was going to need a lot more adrenalin to get through the next two and a half weeks. I'd managed to work out the picture sequences we'd need to shoot in Canberra, but there were still subsidiary interviews to be finalised and filming requirements to be set in place in other parts of Australia. Moreover, this was a constantly evolving story and almost daily there was another rumour or development to unravel. Thank goodness for trusty Kristine, who followed up on a lot of leads and tied up countless loose ends.

The bulk of the story was filmed by Laurence McManus with sound recordist Ross Byrne. When it comes to pictures, Laurence is a genius. He, more than anyone else, developed the cinematic style that has become a hallmark of *Australian Story*. Ross, too, is a total professional, both a brilliant 'soundo' and a brilliant 'techo'. I was very glad they were available for this challenging shoot.

We were obviously dealing with a very big story, but I can honestly say I never felt overwhelmed. There was a constant cacophony of relevant newspaper, radio and television reports to catch up on at the hotel very early in the mornings and again at night, but for most of the day Laurence, Ross and I were quarantined from the media mayhem going on outside as we filmed in the peaceful grounds of Yarralumla. Besides, if any major newsbreaks occurred I knew I could rely on Deb, Kris or one of my other colleagues to get a message through.

Of course, nothing was ever going to be easy for Dr Hollingworth. In secular Australia, a clergyman as Governor-General had been a contentious issue from the outset. Whilst many people like myself were simply curious to see how this church-state nexus would work out, there were those who were bitterly opposed. Even Peter Hollingworth himself had grappled with how he'd be addressed, deeming the terms 'Bishop' and 'Mr' as unsuitable, and settling finally on 'Dr' when a 'Lambeth Degree' in recognition of his past work was bestowed upon him by the Archbishop of Canterbury in May, just before his investiture. The fact that he'd been appointed by a conservative Prime Minister to represent a monarchy, in the aftermath of a controversial and unsuccessful referendum on becoming a republic, was another millstone. There was anger in some quarters that the PM had missed the opportunity to install our first female Governor-General. And to cap it off, he was following in the footsteps of Sir William Deane, a well-loved exemplar in the role. In many respects, he'd been handed a poisoned chalice.

Although I'd allowed a full day for the interview with Dr Hollingworth, there was no way I could comprehensively cover every criticism that had been levelled at him. The most unwieldy area was the large number of serious sexual abuse cases that had surfaced from his time as Archbishop of Brisbane, involving accusations of mishandling and of siding with perpetrators rather than victims. Now it was necessary to decide which of the cases to home in on forensically and which to canvass more lightly. The Toowoomba Prep School case was obviously the top priority, but nothing was clear-cut about most of the other cases and there was a multitude of factors to contend with including legal and other constraints as well as insufficient or unreliable information.

We'd scheduled the first couple of days at Yarralumla for filming the Governor-General in various situations, which gave me the opportunity to speak informally with him during camera breaks. By the end of the second day I'd managed to elicit the information I needed, but for some reason I had an uneasy feeling that something was eluding me. While Laurence, Ross and I were packing up the camera gear, I asked Dr Hollingworth point blank if there were any other potentially controversial sexual abuse cases from his time as archbishop that hadn't yet been made public. He started talking, rather dismissively, about a case that he thought might 'fire up'. He said it would be improper for him to name the parties involved, but told of a bishop and a woman who'd had a 'love affair' in a country town in the 1950s, when the bishop was a young priest and the woman was about sixteen or seventeen — he didn't know much about the woman but said she'd been living in a hostel and he thought she might still have been at high school, or possibly had a job. He said the 'love affair' broke up and both married other people, and then many years later the 'love affair' resumed but it didn't work out and the woman was very bitter. He was adamant that it was not a case of sexual abuse, and also expressed concern that the situation had been very difficult for the bishop's wife.

I'd read a single, rather old and very brief reference to a case that seemed vaguely similar, but it had never resurfaced. Added to that, the Governor-General had certainly spoken convincingly, in a way that he hadn't about other cases. So, *prima facie*, it didn't seem particularly volatile compared to everything else that was in question. I added the new details to my case list, but didn't really think much more about it.

The remainder of the Yarralumla shoot was completed smoothly. I raced off to catch a plane to Melbourne where I met up with another camera crew, Trevor Moore and Colin Swan, leaving Laurence and Ross in Canberra to film some 'pick ups' — additional pictures not involving the Hollingworths. At this stage we actually had three teams hard at work as I'd also emailed Kris and our very talented Brisbane crew, Anthony Sines and Marc Smith, with a list of pictures we'd need to cover Dr Hollingworth's time as Archbishop of Brisbane as well as shots to illustrate the Toowoomba and other cases.

The main purpose of the Melbourne trip was to interview Deborah Hollingworth, the Governor-General's eldest daughter. Deborah is a lawyer who was working in legal aid, and everything about her manner and surroundings suggested a very caring person with a strong sense of social justice. I liked her immensely. She was clearly troubled by the turmoil engulfing her father, whom she loved very dearly, but she was not unrealistic about his short-comings. The father she described was a very hardworking and principled man. For twenty-five years he'd distinguished himself as a social worker and eventually executive director of the Brotherhood of St Laurence welfare organisation, being widely admired for his outspoken advocacy on behalf of the disadvantaged and for bringing the problems of poverty into the public domain. Where Deborah felt huge misgivings was in relation to his move to Brisbane and the fundamental change to his role in the church. As archbishop he was thrown into a world of pomp and ceremony, a world that required him to administer what was essentially akin to a huge business corporation, a world that he embraced but for which he was not skilled.

Whilst those with whom Peter Hollingworth had worked at the Brotherhood were not unanimously effusive in their praise of him, it was certainly in Brisbane that the rot set in. His positive initiatives, such as introducing a welfare focus and supporting the ordination of women, were completely overshadowed by a torrent of criticism that grew ever more vehement with his ascension to the vice-regal role. Deborah could not recognise her father in some of the reports, variously describing him as 'arrogant, uncaring, lacking compassion, self-seeking, an establishment person, a silver tail, a self-promoter' and even one she recalled that began 'Peter Hollingworth must be the vainest person in Australia'. By contrast, household staff at Yarralumla had been enthusiastically positive, telling me of his warmth towards them and in that regard comparing him more than favourably with his virtually 'sainted' predecessor, Sir William Deane. But, there was little time to ruminate on such matters.

Back in Sydney, our editor Ian Harley had begun gearing up. We'd been in touch during the shoot and discussed the opening picture sequence, and by the time I burst through the door with the Canberra tapes late on Tuesday afternoon, 5 February, he'd already selected a perfect piece of music. When it comes to editing, there isn't anyone I so totally trust as Ian. His filmic sense and judgement is always 'frame perfect' in both vision and sound, and he has a marvellous mix of intellect and creativity.

We needed to complete our editing by the following Wednesday in order to meet the post-production schedule and have sufficient time for final legal and editorial checks. This meant we had to start editing pretty much straight away. The only problem was, I had yet to structure and write the script.

Dubs of the interview tapes had been made in Canberra and sent off to typists and fortunately the transcripts were now starting to come through so I stayed at home to write, working pretty much nonstop with barely time for sleep or showers and sustained only by my husband Bruno supplying food and endless cuppas. Luckily, I'd managed to log the picture sequences on a portable viewing machine in my hotel room at night, but I still needed to make final selections of archival material and also look at the interviews — transcripts really only give you an idea of the content and it's necessary to actually see the tapes to select the right 'moments'. With a program like ours, where the narrative is told exclusively from the interviews, this 'viewing' is a time-consuming task.

Meantime, executive producer Deborah Fleming was also going through the transcripts and had decided, quite rightly, that Dr Hollingworth's candour warranted extra airtime for the story. This added greatly to both Ian's and my workload — not that we were complaining, though it would be an understatement to say that the pressure was really on now!

Until this stage, we'd kept the fact that we were filming with the Governor-General under wraps. If ever we'd had the slightest doubt about the furore surrounding him, it was certainly wiped away when Deb authorised a press release about our upcoming program. The entire media went wild. A quote of just twelve words — 'If they feel that I let them down, well then I did' — was bandied around the country and analysed by people who had absolutely no idea of the context. It was, after all, just a press release and intended as nothing more than a tantalising piece of advertising! Then a plethora of commentators opined that *Australian Story* was 'too soft' or otherwise inappropriate to have been granted the interview with the Governor-General. It was extraordinary stuff! Luckily I have both a sense of humour and an exceptionally supportive boss — Deb, of course, was the only other journalist who knew what was in the interview and considered it anything but 'soft'.

Amidst these absurd conditions, I started to drip-feed a script through to Deb and Ian by fax. Somehow we got through it all by Wednesday 13 February, and the completed story was sent to Deb in our Brisbane head office that evening. There was, however, no chance to be complacent. Since our press release, revelations about Dr Hollingworth had been unpacking at an accelerating pace and we'd gotten wind that the well-respected Channel 9 *Sunday* program was working on a scathing story about his time as Archbishop of Brisbane.

I happened to be at our Brisbane studios on the Friday, helping with the super-imposing of captions and other finishing touches to our program, when confirmation came through that the *Sunday* report was being rushed to air the coming weekend, a day before our own program. Although we were pretty confident we'd covered the general territory in our story, we realised we'd probably have to do a partial re-cut to directly respond to whatever specific accusations emerged. I'd come to Brisbane just for the day, but it seemed sensible that I stay, especially as we knew Dr Hollingworth himself was scheduled to arrive there sometime Sunday. So I went off to buy some extra clothes and emergency toiletries, while Ian packed up camera tapes in Sydney and sent them up on the next flight.

I was none too pleased at this development for reasons quite unrelated; namely, I had long-standing social commitments for Saturday night. In fact, I was still seriously considering making a rush trip to Sydney and back, but a combination of Deb's good commonsense — pointing out that I was already exhausted — and the front page headline in Saturday morning's *Sydney Morning Herald* put paid to any idea of that.

Under the headline 'G-g spared sex-abuse bishop', journalist Greg Roberts outlined a case that began in a country hostel in the 1950s when the bishop was a young priest, pretty much identical to the story Dr Hollingworth had told me two weeks earlier, except that instead of a 'love affair' with a girl aged sixteen or seventeen it claimed repeated sexual abuse from the age of fourteen. No one was identified and scant other information was available to us, despite attempts to find out more.

The allegations in John Lyons' report on the *Sunday* program next day were also very strong, though pretty much as we'd expected. He did not include anything about the case revealed in the *Herald*, but had damning testimonies from other victims.

The combined weight of the two reports was such that Deb Fleming and I decided we should try to re-interview the Governor-General. So we worked the phones and after a lot of to-ing and fro-ing and lengthy discussions, we finally arranged for myself, cameraman Anthony Sines and sound recordist Marc Smith to meet with Dr Hollingworth at his hotel late that afternoon.

Obviously, the only way to tackle this interview was to ask him to respond to each and every one of the newly aired allegations. I was quite taken aback by the complete change in the Governor-General's demeanour. He was in a corner and he knew it, but he was fighting with considerable hubris.

It was the *Sunday* program that seemed to have particularly rattled Dr Hollingworth but, as so often happens, his nemesis would come in the form of the question least likely.

I asked him to tell me his reaction to the allegations in the *Sydney Morning Herald* article and give his version of the case involving the bishop and the woman, as he'd told me before. His answer was as follows:

I think there was a headline over the weekend in the *Sydney Morning Herald* that said, 'G-g spares sex abuse bishop'. Now that is a headline grabber, isn't it? Behind all this lies a human tragedy, both for the woman concerned and for the bishop and his family. I have tried to deal with that issue for many years now, and my predecessor likewise. This is something that happened over forty years ago. A young priest and a young woman, in a church run hostel in the country, my belief is that this was not sex abuse, there was no suggestion of rape or anything like that, quite the contrary. My information is that it was rather the other way round, and I don't want to say any more than that, but I can tell you that we made every effort we could to try and find a professional mediation. It wasn't possible. I feel deeply sad for the woman concerned. The fact is, of course, that it was a relationship that was sporadic over all those years. It was resumed much later, and I believe the bishop, who has been long retired, long retired, and who is living in the diocese, and his wife and family, have resolved all this among themselves. But we can't settle it with the lady concerned; to my great sadness she's taken it to the newspapers, and I don't know what good that does.

The words 'a young priest and a young woman' were somewhat vague and misleading. Dr Hollingworth had previously told me the girl was sixteen or seventeen, but the *Herald* article had said 'she was abused repeatedly over two years from the age of fourteen'. In a climate in which every word the Governor-General uttered would be under intense scrutiny, it was clearly necessary to address the discrepancy to establish whether or not the girl was under the age of consent as the newspaper inferred.

When I stopped the camera to sort this out, a rather spirited discussion about the issue ensued between Dr Hollingworth and his official secretary, Martin Bonsey, who was sitting in on the interview. Eventually Dr Hollingworth seemed to be conceding that the girl was fifteen years of age when the sexual liaison began, and the discussion turned to whether the age of consent was fourteen or sixteen. It was sixteen, but the Governor-General seemed reluctant to accept that. There was also talk of the times being different in the 1950s and that girls left school and got married much earlier than they do today, so relationships at an early age weren't out of the ordinary.

It was a very strange situation. Dr Hollingworth did not contradict or want to revise his previous answer, quite the reverse, so we agreed that all we needed to do was clarify the girl's age, although I suggested he might wish to repeat the whole thing, beginning with his introductory remarks about the claims in the *Herald*. He chose to simply clarify the girl's age:

> The great tragedy about this situation is that the genesis of it was forty years ago and it occurred between a young priest and a teenage girl who was under the age of consent. I believe she was more than fourteen and I also understand that many years later in adult life their relationship resumed and it was partly a pastoral relationship and it was partly something more.

It was already dark when I arrived back at the ABC studios in Toowong with the new tapes. Deb, supervising producer Ben Hawke, editor Kent Gordon and a team of production assistants and typists were waiting. I'd rung ahead and told Deb what Dr Hollingworth had said, and she and Ben had organised to send a couple of the interview grabs to our newsroom for the 7 o'clock bulletin, so there was a mad rush to locate them on the tapes. As well, Ben was working on a 'highlights package' from our original story, which together with some of the new interview would be sent out to the rest of the media.

Deb, meantime, had also called management who'd given the okay to extend the program by fifteen minutes — an unprecedented decision — and, together with Ben, she'd identified another two or three minutes that we could cut from the original story. So, we now had about eighteen minutes of sensitive, potentially explosive story to cut by the morning — a very big ask. This was no time to panic. The sensible approach was to run the allegations followed by Dr Hollingworth's responses. So, after discussion with Deb and a call to our lawyer, Kent and I started hacking into a dub of the *Sunday* program while Anthony filmed the front page of the *Sydney Morning Herald*.

As the transcripts came in from the typists, Deb and I went through them with a fine-tooth comb and we both identified a number of Dr Hollingworth's answers that would probably fuel debate. For instance, I remember Anthony and Marc expressing their utter astonishment about what the Governor-General had said about the priest and the teenage girl. On the other hand, it didn't seem especially out of character for a man of his generation who prided himself on seeing the 'grey' of situations and forgiving those who transgressed the church's or indeed society's rules.

By midnight, only Kent and I remained, and we began to assemble the final program. I'd created a script of sorts by spreading transcript pages across the floor and highlighting the sections of the interview that were pertinent. At about 3 am Kent managed to get an hour or so of sleep while I sorted out a few remaining 'holes' in the edit, including the *Herald* case. Having worked on sexual abuse stories previously, I felt some unease that I had been unable to speak with the woman involved or find out any further details or confirm those that had been provided. However, I was convinced that the Governor-General believed the relationship had been a long-running 'love affair' that had gone sour and that in his view sexual abuse was never involved.

The edited version was:

[*The initial introductory line.*] I think there was a headline over the weekend in the Sydney Morning Herald that said, 'G-g spares sex abuse bishop'. Now, that is a headline grabber, isn't it? [*Then the clarification.*] The great tragedy about this situation is that the genesis of it was forty years ago and it occurred between a young priest and a teenage girl who was under the age of consent.
I believe she was more than fourteen and I also understand that many years later in adult life, their relationship resumed and it was partly a pastoral relationship and it was partly something more. [*Then his answer regarding the alleged sexual abuse.*] My belief is that this was not sex abuse. There was no suggestion of rape or anything like that. Quite the contrary, my information is that it was rather the other way around. And I don't want to say any more than that.

By 8 am, the re-edit was done.

But, there were still a few loose ends to tie up. Among them, Dr Hollingworth had told me he'd spoken with the bishop at the centre of the *Sydney Morning Herald* storm and expected him to release a statement to the media that would 'clear it all up'. Sure enough, articles appeared in Monday morning's *Herald* and also Brisbane's *Courier Mail* naming Bishop Donald Shearman, though not the woman. Bishop Shearman echoed Dr Hollingworth, rejecting the term 'sex abuse' and being similarly equivocal about the girl's age. Frankly, I had no way of knowing who was telling the truth.

Later in the morning, one of my colleagues took a call from the Governor-General's office, seeking to provide clarifications and factual corrections to a couple of his answers relating to other cases. It was all material that we had in any case excluded from the final edit but, significantly in view of what was soon to develop, there was no mention at all of any problems with what he'd said regarding Bishop Shearman. Our program ran that night. I had not slept for thirty-eight hours.

The media, of course, leaped onto a great many of Dr Hollingworth's assertions, and various aspects of our story dominated newspapers, radio and television. Some of the commentary, especially on talkback radio, was nothing short of hysterical — facts were quoted incorrectly and there was an ugly predilection to play the man rather than the ball.

Surprisingly, it was a couple of days before attention turned to the one comment that Dr Hollingworth and many others believe triggered his final downfall.

Initially, as Deb and I had predicted, opinion was divided over his remarks about Bishop Shearman and the girl, with perhaps the most forceful comments coming from those who agreed with Dr Hollingworth. It was in this climate that, on Wednesday 20 February, prominent academic and businesswoman Wendy McCarthy spoke out strongly. Wendy, it transpired, had not only been a boarder at the country hostel where the abuse by the then 'Padre' Shearman took place, she'd shared a dormitory and bunk bed with the girl. Apart from confirming that the girl was indeed under age, Wendy revealed that Padre Shearman was married at the time of the abuse and also the warden in charge of, and taking parental responsibility for, the children at the hostel. I was gobsmacked — in other words, he was both an adulterer and *in loco parentis*! As well, I'd discovered that Donald Shearman was nearly thirty at the time — considerably older than I had previously been led to believe — and I would later learn that he already had a child.

Meanwhile, the Governor-General had been under such pressure over a range of issues that he'd prepared an official 'Statement' in answer to his various critics. In this document — also released on the Wednesday — he states that 'Retired Bishop Shearman had sex with a girl of about 15 years of age when he was a young curate some 50 years ago'. He acknowledges that the then Padre Shearman was supervising the hostel where the girl was resident and says he does not condone and has never condoned Shearman having had sex with her. Noticeably, however, he falls short of directly acknowledging that Shearman was *in loco parentis*, nor does he acknowledge 'sexual abuse' or carnal knowledge as a criminal offence. More glaringly, he omits to mention that the so-called 'young curate' was already married — and had a child — so had therefore committed adultery as well. He does not apologise to the woman, nor, again significantly, does he suggest any problem with how he was represented on *Australian Story*, although he did correct himself on comments he'd made on the program about another case.

Wendy McCarthy's comments had thrown more fuel on to what was fast becoming the Hollingworth pyre. His Statement was examined and compared mercilessly with his previous utterances. The following day, Thursday 21 February — three days after our broadcast — a panicky Governor-General gave an impromptu 'doorstop' comment to the media throng gathered outside Yarralumla about what he'd said on our program:

> I want to say something else as well which I believe is very, very important and I'm very upset about myself. On the *Australian Story* on Monday night I answered a question. I think I didn't hear the question properly or something like that. It gave the impression that I was: a) condoning child abuse, sex child abuse, and secondly that I was really talking about a girl. I thought I was talking about an adult relationship. And I want to make an unreserved apology to the woman concerned and to the whole of the Australian public. That was not what I meant and I realise that particular little segment has been picked up and used on the media yesterday. Had I known, and had I had the opportunity, I would have rectified it in the Statement that I made.

His words, 'I didn't hear the question properly or something like that', could not have been more provocative. Within minutes, pressure was on us from the rest of the media to release the unedited camera tape and management ordered us to do so.

I wonder if any camera tape in the recent history of Australian television has ever been scrutinised by so many people. It was a disaster for Dr Hollingworth. The unanimous view of commentators — on television and radio that evening and across the front pages of newspapers the next day, and beyond — was that he had been represented fairly, perhaps even too fairly. Indeed, the release of the camera tape made his situation worse because it showed beyond doubt that he was talking directly and only about the abuse at the hostel when the girl was fifteen, whereas what we had put to air arguably also incorporated the adult affair.

Ultimately, Peter Hollingworth was a victim of himself. When I'd re-interviewed him on Sunday 17 February, I had precious little information available to me. I didn't know the names of the individuals involved, or that the priest was married, or that he was *in loco parentis* at the hostel, or that he already had a child. Nor was this information available to me from the church. Later I discovered that Dr Hollingworth had access to all of this information. These new facts, of course, put the issue of the girl's age into a different perspective: whether or not she was under the age of consent was significant in terms of criminality, but expert opinion decrees that this situation was 'sexual abuse' regardless of the age — fourteen, fifteen, sixteen or seventeen — because Donald Shearman

Producer Helen Grasswill, sound recordist Ross Byrne and cameraman Laurence McManus filming with Dr Hollingworth and his wife Ann at the Governor-General's official Sydney residence.

was a married priest who betrayed the power and trust vested in him by his church as well as the responsibility he had in taking the place of the girl's parents by virtue of his position as warden of the hostel. It's also worth noting that subsequent sexual contact in adult life is widely accepted as an extension of the original abuse in cases such as this because of the insidious bond that abusers create with their young victims, through promises and lies, and the consequent power they hold over them.

Early the following Monday morning, 25 February, I received a phone call at home from Dr Hollingworth, triggered by the publication that day of my response to criticism directed at *Australian Story* in a weekend newspaper. A columnist had implied that we'd been too lenient on the Governor-General by not running his original comment about the girl at the hostel. On the contrary, of course, it was our edit that made it clear the girl was under age and not a 'young woman' of indeterminate age.

I do not recall Peter Hollingworth asking for this phone conversation to be 'off the record', but I have chosen to regard the details of it as such. In general terms, however, I suppose the call could be characterised as an exercise in 'soul searching' on his part. What I will say, because it is relevant to a debate that has continued, is that Dr Hollingworth told me he felt that he 'could not have had a fairer interviewer'. It was a striking phrase in the circumstances and I mentioned to Deb at the time that he had used it.

Dr Hollingworth had met the woman at the centre of this controversial case only once, in 1995, when he was archbishop and she'd come to a mediation in Brisbane wearing a purple bishop's shirt and an episcopal ring, both given to her by Bishop Shearman after he renewed contact when she was an adult. It must have made a considerable impression. I found myself wondering if perhaps, for some reason, Dr Hollingworth could never see beyond this angry 55-year-old woman he'd actually met to the innocent fourteen and fifteen-year-old girl she had once been.

In his letter of apology to the woman on 1 March 2002, he shows a new understanding:

What happened to you as a girl at the hostel was wrong and you were in no way responsible for it. I am deeply sorry for the words I used on *Australian Story* that suggested otherwise. I cannot try to explain or excuse them. All that matters to me now is that you should be aware of how sorry I am. There is little now that I can do but to express once again my apology and my regret for all that you have been through, in the past and in the present. I cannot change the past but if I could, what I wish most of all is that you never had to suffer the pain and anguish associated with the things that have happened to you over the years.

Typewritten briefing notes for a subsequent face-to-face meeting between Dr Hollingworth and the woman on Sunday 24 March 2002, indicate an even greater willingness to admit to and learn from past mistakes. His comment on *Australian Story* was now being described as 'shameful' and a 'terrible thing' to have said. There was a recognition that he 'must take full responsibility for the words and for the understandable criticism they generated in the broader community'. The notes also suggest that he had gained a sense that in his previous role as archbishop he had some difficulty in identifying and acknowledging the feelings of victims of sexual abuse, and that this was an area in which he wanted to do better. And he seemed to now recognise that what Donald Shearman had done to the woman as a schoolgirl was 'a terrible betrayal of trust'.

It so happens that I have known Wendy McCarthy for about twenty years and have enormous respect for her. After she blew the whistle on this sorry affair, I contacted her with a view to putting the whole story on the record. Over the next three years I learnt a great deal more about this case, culminating in early 2005 with a two-part *Australian Story* in which the woman, Beth Heinrich, identified herself publicly for the first time. Her story was gut-wrenching. Her life had been absolutely devastated in the wake of Donald Shearman's sexual exploitation and horrific betrayal of her — all wrapped up in talk of love, promises of marriage and a good deal of brainwashing 'God spin'.

Apart from the historical perspective, the case offered a rare opportunity to examine the 'anatomy' of sexual abuse and hopefully provide further understanding of this difficult, complex and widespread problem in our society. By this stage Donald Shearman had been stripped of his holy orders by an Anglican tribunal, which in August 2004 found he'd committed offences against the church relating to his sexual abuse of Beth Heinrich. However, he had refused to appear before either this tribunal or a major church inquiry in 2003, which also ruled against him, and had offered no apology to Beth Heinrich. Peter Hollingworth had continued on as Governor-General for another fifteen months following the broadcast of our program, enduring ongoing criticism and an unsubstantiated allegation of rape brought against him by a woman who later suicided. It was a hideously rough trot, exacerbated by worry about his wife, Ann, who was struggling with breast cancer; hardly surprisingly, he'd been diagnosed with clinical depression. His resignation eventually came on 28 May 2003 after the release of the inquiry report, which censured aspects of his handling of sexual abuse complaints while Archbishop of Brisbane. Since then he'd been attempting to redeem himself, with some success, by learning more about sexual abuse and trying to contribute positively where he could.

So, when we started to film Beth Heinrich's story, we had some hope that Dr Hollingworth might agree to participate — perhaps in the spirit of healing and reconciliation that he had been recently describing. We also approached Donald Shearman, though with less optimism given his previous refusal to give any explanation of his

Beth Heinrich, whose fight for justice triggered the final downfall of former Governor-General Dr Peter Hollingworth.

behaviour to the inquiry or tribunal. I spoke by phone with both men, but unfortunately they declined to participate in the program.

Beth Heinrich, nevertheless, had a right to tell her story, which was well corroborated by a breathtaking 'audit trail' of some 300 'love letters' written by Donald Shearman himself, as well as reams of documents. There were also letters to Beth from Archbishop Hollingworth that shocked me and demonstrated a response to her that was insensitive at the very least. The earliest of these letters was written following the 1995 mediation, which he had attended as an observer. At this time, Beth's much loved only son had just died and her grief, combined with extenuating circumstances involving Bishop Shearman, undoubtedly had a bearing on her emotional state. She certainly felt disbelieved and that the church had abandoned her.

In an ABC radio interview in mid-2004 and again in a *Bulletin* magazine article in May 2005, Dr Hollingworth made claims that have continued to upset Beth Heinrich. She says she particularly objects to his assertion that as archbishop he tried very hard to resolve her troubles, when she believes — with justification — that he did not. As well, she was deeply hurt and angered by some of Dr Hollingworth's submissions to the 2003 inquiry. For Beth, these developments have made Peter Hollingworth's previous apology seem hollow. She and her supporters feel that he still does not 'get it' and should revise his position unequivocally. But more importantly, Beth says she needs the perpetrator of the abuse, Donald Shearman, to totally vindicate her and apologise. Experts in this difficult field say such acknowledgement is crucial for healing.

Strangely, in these recent interviews and elsewhere, Peter Hollingworth has also revived the old innuendo that it was our editing process — not his own comments — that caused so much public controversy in 2002. His assertion now is that the interview was stopped in order to clarify the question being asked and to enable him to give a less ambiguous answer, and that he then gave a completely new answer and expected the original one to be expunged.

Whilst it is understandable that Dr Hollingworth wishes to clear his name, and the situation was certainly complicated, there were, of course, others present — one of his staff and our camera crew. I can confidently reiterate that there was neither an undertaking nor any request to delete or discard the substance of the original response, which comprised the only time Dr Hollingworth gave an answer to the allegation that this was a case of sexual abuse. Nor was there ever any suggestion that his opinion was other than that this was *not* a case of sexual abuse. It simply was not an issue at this point, and, moreover, even if it had been raised as an issue, ABC editorial guidelines both allow and require us to use our editorial discretion in relation to what to omit and what to include, within the bounds of fairness and accuracy. We did not set out to prosecute a case against him, nor would we conspire with him: we simply reported accurately what he said.

In the recent *Bulletin* article, Peter Hollingworth lamented the ongoing humiliation of his situation and pointed to a 'deeply virulent, secularist, anti-religious streak out there in Australian society' as contributing to the media and public backlash against him. Perhaps, but some of his fiercest critics are from within the Anglican Church itself. In particular, these critics question Dr Hollingworth's judgement in continuing to strongly support Donald Shearman, whom he describes as a man who is 'profoundly penitent', and they point out that whilst it is admirable that he does not turn his back on the 'sinner' he needs also to recognise that penitence is not enough without adequate reparation to the victim.

If Peter Hollingworth truly wants to get this 'monkey' off his back, as he told the *Bulletin*, many believe he could make a good start by encouraging his friend Donald Shearman to offer an unconditional public apology to Beth Heinrich. Perhaps then, people might believe he has faced his own demons, and embrace him again.

As the producer of this *Australian Story* that was so significant and fateful for Peter Hollingworth, I did not find that he was the ogre some have painted him to be. For me, the tragedy is that an otherwise well-meaning man seems still to have been unable to come to terms with the complex underlying issues that led to his terrible fall from grace.

Kirsty Sword and Xanana Gusmao at their wedding in Dili in 2000.

Dangerous Liaison

Ben Cheshire

When 'Dangerous Liaison' aired on *Australian Story* in February 2002, Kirsty Sword Gusmao was about to become First Lady of the newly independent East Timor. It was a remarkable turnaround for the former Melbourne ballet student who had worked as an undercover agent for the East Timorese resistance before falling in love with East Timorese leader Xanana Gusmao, who was then in gaol in Jakarta.

Producer Ben Cheshire corresponded with Kirsty Sword Gusmao for more than a year before getting the green light to make the program, which later became a finalist in the 2002 New York Festivals, a prestigious international television award.

The walls of the Cipinang Prison in Jakarta were high and imposing. Above the whitewashed concrete slabs, coils of razor-sharp barbed wire separated the prisoners from the relentless traffic outside. We were there to film the cell where East Timorese leader Xanana Gusmao had been locked up for seven years. As I climbed the stairs to meet the prison director, cameraman Quentin Davis was a few steps behind me, secretly filming the object in my hand — a woman's handbag.

It was a bizarre moment; part of a carefully planned re-enactment of the method that had been used to smuggle items to Gusmao.

In the director's office, we sipped cups of tea and attempted a conversation conducted mostly through smiles and sign language since he spoke little English and my Indonesian was non-existent. Then the prison guards took us to see Gusmao's former cell, inside a compound reserved for East Timorese political prisoners. It was here we hoped to complete the sequence of shots that would illustrate the smuggling story. To my relief, the guards were cooperative.

Would they mind showing us how gifts had been delivered to Gusmao? No problem. How about demonstrating the procedure, using the handbag I had brought with me? Sure.

After a cursory examination by a supervisor, the handbag was waved through.

Kirsty Sword, an Australian who had led a double life as an aid worker and activist for the East Timorese resistance in the early 1990s, had told us how she had managed to send packages to Gusmao. It seemed a little bribery went a long way.

Xanana came to know of my presence in Jakarta, and when he knew that I had access to things like email, he started to write to me and ask whether I would be a conduit for information and correspondence. Basically the correspondence to and from the prison was thanks to the eminently corruptible nature of the guards who worked in this high-security prison. Salaries were extremely low, so people were very open to doing extracurricular activities, including couriering letters in and out of the prison.

I had bought the handbag a few days before, in the markets of the East Timorese capital, Dili. We had filmed Kirsty packing it with letters and even a mobile phone, as she had done on one occasion. Now, after filming in the prison itself, we had the beginning and end of an intriguing sequence that would demonstrate one of the more daring exploits of 'Ruby Blade', Kirsty's alter ego as undercover agent for the East Timorese resistance movement.

Producer Ben Cheshire (left) and cameraman Quentin Davis attract the curiosity of the local kids outside a burnt-out building in Dili.

In the seven years since that time, Kirsty Sword had married Xanana Gusmao and become First Lady of a newly independent East Timor. It was a truly remarkable story. As everybody kept saying, it sounded like the plot of a movie or romance novel, but it was all true.

Just as dramatic was East Timor's transformation from Indonesia's twenty-seventh province to fledgling independent state. Indonesian forces had invaded the country in 1975, just days after the departure of the Portuguese who had colonised the island for more than 400 years. The main East Timorese independence movement, Fretilin, led by Xanana Gusmao, began a rebel campaign to oust the Indonesians. In 1990, up to 180 East Timorese were killed when Indonesian soldiers fired on protestors at the Santa Cruz cemetery in what became known as the Dili massacre.

This was a turning point for Kirsty Sword, then employed as a researcher and interpreter on a British television documentary that exposed the massacre to the world. She packed her bags and went to Jakarta, resolved to use the skills she had acquired in a 'privileged background' in Melbourne (where she had once considered a career as a ballet dancer) to help the East Timorese cause. By day Kirsty Sword was an English teacher and development officer for an Australian aid agency. By night, she was the secret agent, Ruby Blade.

> Everyone involved in the clandestine movement had a code name or pseudonym, which was only known to other members of the clandestine movement. I adopted Ruby Blade — Blade because it was something like Sword, and Ruby just because it sounded kind of Agatha Christie.

Xanana Gusmao returns to Dili after seven years in gaol.

Kirsty had to keep her two worlds completely separate. The only connection was that by doing one job, she was able to support herself to do the other. The undercover work was dangerous. If discovered by Indonesian military intelligence, she would have faced deportation, gaol or worse. Some East Timorese activists simply disappeared. At the time, many people in the west regarded East Timorese independence as a lost cause. A more pressing priority was to maintain good relations with Indonesia, a country with the largest Islamic population in the world.

In 1992, the East Timorese independence movement suffered a major setback when Xanana Gusmao was captured outside Dili and imprisoned in Jakarta.

As it turned out, that's where the paths of Kirsty Sword and Xanana Gusmao finally crossed. After corresponding initially by letter and later by mobile phone, Kirsty arranged a trip to Cipinang Prison in 1994 under the pretence of visiting her 'uncle', an Australian who was in prison for fraud. During the visit, she was able to spend some time with Xanana and, just like in the movies, they fell in love. But four years were to pass before they saw each other again.

In 1999, after the fall of Indonesia's President Suharto, new President B J Habibie announced a referendum would be held in East Timor to allow the East Timorese to choose between independence or autonomy within Indonesia. Seventy-eight per cent of the people voted for independence, triggering a campaign of terror by pro-Indonesian militia groups. As many as 1000 East Timorese were killed and all major buildings in Dili were destroyed.

Like many Australians at the time, I recall listening with horror to the news from East Timor. Each day there were stories of further atrocities. Hundreds of people were reported to be seeking refuge in the United Nations compound in Dili while murder and mayhem went on around them. It seemed crazy that the rest of the world was doing nothing to help them.

Eventually, the Indonesian government allowed a 7500-strong peacekeeping force, led by Australia, to re-establish order in East Timor. Xanana Gusmao was released from gaol and returned to Dili where he received a hero's welcome. Twenty-four hours later he was joined by Kirsty.

After a while, the torrent of news from East Timor slowed to a trickle. I was being kept busy making programs for *Australian Story* and had no idea that events would conspire to take me to that country. Then, in November 2000, Doug Sleeman, an ABC News cameraman, dropped into my office in a state of great excitement.

'You should have a look at this tape. This woman would make a great *Australian Story*,' he said.

Doug had just come back from filming a speech given by Kirsty Sword Gusmao at Parliament House in Sydney. She was accompanied by her baby son, Alexandre, then just a few weeks old, and while Kirsty spoke the baby was cuddled by Lynne Cosgrove, wife of Lieutenant General Peter Cosgrove who had commanded the Australian forces in East Timor. Kirsty wept as she spoke of her joy at having a child in a free East Timor.

> My roots are now firmly anchored in East Timor, in a country I love and have passionately fought for, with the people that I also love and have fought for. My son, Alexandre, here with me, is a son of East Timorese soil. And to be able to give birth to him in a free and independent East Timor was, for Xanana and me, the icing on the cake of a very long and hard-won struggle.

The story aired that night on the ABC's *Lateline* program but, having seen the tape, I was already hooked. It was hard to imagine a more fascinating subject for *Australian Story*. Even at that early stage it appeared likely that Xanana Gusmao would run for President whenever the elections were held in East Timor. That would make Kirsty the First Lady of Australia's newest neighbour. But would Kirsty be interested in talking to us? Margherita Tracanelli, a friend of Kirsty's, agreed to sound her out on our behalf.

In February 2001 I received the following email:

> Dear Ben
> Margherita had spoken to me some time ago about your interest in doing something on me and my work for East Timor over the years. I cannot claim to feel anything like a worthy subject, but I do very much like your program and the approach it takes.
> I would like very much to have a talk with you by phone and suggest that tomorrow at about 11 am Dili time (1 pm Sydney time) might be good for me. I hope this is not encroaching too much on your lunch hour!
> Warm regards,
> Kirsty Sword Gusmao.

So began almost a year of phone calls, emails and frustrating delays as we tried to find mutually convenient dates for a possible *Australian Story* trip to East Timor. In the meantime, I researched Kirsty's background by speaking to people who had known her in her earlier life. It seemed everybody had a story to tell about her and, most promisingly, some people had snippets of home video of Kirsty in her various guises as ballet dancer, foreign aid worker and secret agent. If I could gather all these bits and pieces, along with Kirsty's own collection plus interviews with key people such as her mother, it had the potential to make a terrific program. By necessity, much of her story had been deliberately kept secret prior to this.

In an email to Kirsty in March 2001, I proposed putting all the material together to portray her complete story for the first time on *Australian Story*. Later, she explained why she decided to take part.

> I don't think I had ever actually seen an episode of *Australian Story*, as I spent so much time abroad throughout the 1990s. However, I had heard good things about it from friends and family members whose opinions I respected. I knew it to be a serious, well-regarded and very candid documentary series, and for reasons of its excellent reputation I agreed to participate in the program.

Six months later, Kirsty and I met face to face when the Gusmaos made a trip to Melbourne. As well as recording interviews with Kirsty and her mother, Rosalie Sword, we were able to pin down a definite date to start filming in East Timor: 10 January 2002.

It was the first time that *Australian Story* would send its own three-person film crew on an overseas shoot — an expensive proposition, but worth it, we thought. Cameraman Quentin Davis, sound recordist Ross Byrne and I began packing our gear and had vaccinations for typhoid, hepatitis A and tetanus.

The budget was tight and getting tighter. Plans to fly Kirsty to Jakarta for a few days to talk about her earlier experiences there had to be abandoned. At the last minute, we managed to save some precious travel dollars by wangling free seats on a United Nations flight from Darwin to Dili. Loaded into the back of a Hercules transport plane, along with crates of supplies and medicine, we finally touched down in East Timor.

It was hot, noisy and chaotic. But fascinating to see the country I had by this time read and heard so much about. Already about a quarter of Dili's main structures had been rebuilt. Nevertheless, entire streets still lay in ruins, the broken buildings pockmarked with bullet holes and black soot from fires.

We drove past the former UN compound and tried to imagine the scene just over two years before, when hundreds of people were crammed into the grounds, seeking refuge from rampaging militia groups. Kirsty also took us to a former political prison, which the new UN Transitional Administration (UNTAET) hoped to transform into the national office of the East Timor Reconciliation Commission.

The Gusmaos' home in the hills overlooking Dili was a picture of calm and tranquillity, if you could ignore the armed bodyguards at the entrance and the ever-present cacophony of noises outside. We quickly discovered that recording interviews there was problematic. Because there is no reporter voice-over on *Australian Story*, it's important to have top-quality sound when people are telling us their stories. It would sound strange if a rooster could be heard crowing in the background when Kirsty was telling us about one of her teenage ballet performances, for example.

The narrow winding street outside the Gusmaos' home was the main road out of Dili, with a constant stream of ancient trucks, motorbikes and minibuses. Because the road was so narrow, drivers honked their horn at every corner to warn approaching traffic. This set off all the local dogs on a barking spree, upsetting the chickens and roosters who started to squawk, almost drowning out the noise from the helicopters frequently flying across the valley.

What we needed was a nice, quiet room where we could sit down with Kirsty for a couple of hours and record our main interview with her. But it seemed there were no nice, quiet rooms in

Dili. Every place we looked at had the same problems. Eventually we zeroed in on the World Bank, where Kirsty had been given a small outside hut from which to run her Alola Foundation for women raped in war. The hut itself was no good for us because of the hum from a large air-conditioning unit next door. But the office of the World Bank's local manager looked just fine, nestled inside a large building that had recently been restored. With a little help from Kirsty, we arranged to use the manager's office after 5 pm, when most of the staff had gone home for the day. And that's where Kirsty told us some more of her amazing story. In an email to me later, she said:

> I recall quite keenly that it felt extremely strange throughout the shoot to be talking openly about my story when I had never considered it to be particularly worthy of treatment in this way. Principally, I saw my participation as a way of keeping East Timor in the hearts and minds of the Australian public. I was also hopeful that, more specifically, I could raise awareness and some concrete support for the causes I am presently involved in, mainly those involving women and children in East Timor.

Xanana Gusmao at his cell in Cipinang Prison, Jakarta.

With Kirsty's interview complete, the next thing was to arrange an interview with Xanana. Not surprisingly, he was a busy man. We filmed him at his office in downtown Dili where there was a constant stream of visitors, each seeking help from the man they saw as the saviour of East Timor. There was no chance of sitting down for an hour or two with him in that location. So we set up our camera and lights in the Gusmaos' living room, hoping the noise outside would not be too distracting.

I expected the interview to be reasonably straightforward, given that Xanana had spoken to journalists dozens of times before. Unfortunately, in all the research I had done for the story, nobody had mentioned that Xanana hates being interviewed in English. It was like pulling teeth! Things got worse when I started asking the more personal questions about the unusual way his relationship with Kirsty had started. The silences grew longer as Xanana shifted uncomfortably in his seat. I struggled to rephrase my questions, wondering whether I was being culturally insensitive or whether Xanana's reticence was perhaps typical of his generation.

Eventually, I decided to bring Kirsty into the picture and interview the two of them side by side. Xanana's mood lifted instantly. They joked about their plans to plant pumpkins and take care of the four cows that had been promised to them, the interaction between them clearly demonstrating their great affection for each other. Finally I had some good material with Xanana! But the interview with him on his own was probably the worst I had conducted in twenty-five years of journalism. Of nearly an hour of tape, we ended up using just twenty-one seconds.

While filming Xanana at his workplace, we ran into Jose Ramos Horta, East Timor's Foreign Minister, who immediately volunteered to be part of the program. We arranged to meet him at his office in the old Governor's building near the waterfront, now headquarters for the UN Transitional Administration.

In a jovial mood, Ramos Horta caught me by surprise when he casually mentioned that, during Xanana's incarceration, he had considered hiring former SAS commandos to break Xanana out of gaol. He had even talked to some British former SAS men, veterans of the war in Bosnia. It was a revelation that I knew would make news in Australia — if it was true.

Later that day I ran it past someone who had been involved in the resistance, who dismissed the idea. But when I asked Kirsty, she confirmed the story.

I'd almost forgotten about it, because it was something that we kept very close to our chest for obvious reasons. But I remember that I was part of the plan in some way — that I would get access to information about the actual plan of the prison, the layout of it, and this would be passed on to these individuals that were going to bust him out of gaol.

Xanana's response was that we had to be patient and do things in the proper way. Indonesia needed to be pushed into a corner diplomatically, and acknowledge the error of its ways if you like. There really wasn't anything to be achieved by him breaking out of prison.

With the interviews complete, and some great pictures of the Gusmao family at work and play, we flew to Jakarta to cover the earlier part of Kirsty's story, when she had been a secret agent for the East Timorese resistance. I planned to begin the program with an anecdote from Kirsty, describing how she had sometimes gate-crashed receptions for visiting Australian parliamentarians and taken them late at night through the back streets of Jakarta to meet with members of the resistance.

We needed some re-enactment pictures to illustrate the story but, because of the tight budget at the ABC, we had been unable to bring Kirsty with us to Jakarta. To get around this, we had filmed her getting into a car at night in Dili, with some close-ups of her giving directions and looking out of the window. None of the shots gave away the fact that we had actually filmed them in Dili. Now, to complete the scene, we mounted the camera inside our rented van in Jakarta and drove around for an hour late at night, gathering shots of main streets in the city. In the edit room back in Australia, we mixed the two sequences together, making it appear that we had filmed Kirsty being driven through Jakarta by night. An old television trick but it saved quite a few dollars of taxpayers' money!

When the finished program went to air in February 2002, Kirsty was delighted to discover a way to watch it in Dili.

The first Australian government representative in East Timor, James Batley, was one of the few people in Dili who had access to Australian TV via satellite, so it was in his home that Xanana, Alexandre and I viewed 'Dangerous Liaison'. Given my criticism of successive Australian government policy on East Timor, I felt a little uncomfortable seeing the program in this company. Nevertheless, James seemed to share our satisfaction with the results.

The program made the news on two separate fronts. As I predicted, the revelation that Jose Ramos Horta had concocted a secret plan to break Xanana Gusmao out of gaol was picked up by radio news and current affairs programs. What I hadn't expected was the controversy caused by Kirsty revealing that she had helped the East Timorese resistance while working for an Australian aid agency in Jakarta.

I had contacted the agency concerned and been told that as long as Kirsty had helped the Timorese in her own time, they had no problem with it, especially since there had been a change of regime in Indonesia since then. But it evidently created hot debate in the foreign affairs field, with one newspaper columnist calling for an inquiry into the activities of Australia's non-government organisations (NGOs) involved in foreign aid. Nevertheless, Kirsty was pleased with the response from viewers.

The feedback was overwhelmingly positive. I received abundant letters from Australians of all walks of life, offering their support and encouragement to me personally and to my work for the Alola Foundation, in the months that followed. I found this tremendously affirming and gratifying. Many of these expressions of solidarity translated later into concrete support for my work for the women and children of Timor-Leste [East Timor].

Kirsty's only regret was that the program was never shown on East Timorese television. Very few East Timorese are aware of the history of her involvement in the country's struggle for independence, she explained. Broadcasting 'Dangerous Liaison' inside the country would have given many people access to her story and to the details of her relationship with their leader. Unfortunately, the ABC was unable to arrange a broadcast in East Timor because the program contained footage from a British documentary on the Dili massacre and copyright clearance for on-selling was prohibitively expensive.

Though I haven't been back to East Timor since making the program, I am amused sometimes to find myself regarded in the ABC as an expert on the place. Every now and then I field a call from a program-maker wanting information or to make contact with the Gusmaos.

Kirsty and I remain in touch. Since the program was aired, she has had two more children in fairly quick succession. All three of her children were born in Dili National Hospital, not just because Kirsty wanted them born on East Timorese soil, but because she did not want to allow herself the luxury of first-world medical facilities when most East Timorese have no such choice. Xanana, of course, did run for President, was elected, and is likely to remain in that position for five or ten years. Only then will the Gusmaos be able to pursue their dream of a quiet life growing pumpkins and looking after cows in the hills overlooking Dili. In the meantime, it seems history has more to ask of them.

Kirsty with her baby Alexandre

Matt Laffan

The Ongoing Journey

Matt Laffan

As the hour of eight approached, I raised my glass to a couple of friends who had gathered in my living room, gave them a smile and sipped my wine. Despite my confident exterior I was pensive with the knowledge that in a few moments a version of my life story was about to be exposed on ABC TV's *Australian Story*, and from that point on it would be irretrievable.

Being a fellow with a physical disability, which by its very nature makes me look different from most people, I am aware that my presence often attracts attention. My short stature and use of an electric wheelchair can take aback the uninitiated. Typically, after I engage folks in conversation and turn to subjects that matter, this reaction dissipates. However, when the program began and my image burst onto the screen, I found myself transfixed by the sight of myself moving, talking and engaging with others. Only television can produce such an out-of-body experience.

I'd met the producer of my story, Ben Cheshire, some six months before. My first face-to-face contact with him was in the Supreme Court of New South Wales. I'd been representing the Office of the Director of Public Prosecutions in a bail application, and turned to see whether Ben was there, as arranged. Behind me were the usual suspects — police, relatives and a journalist — and one fellow who was set apart from the rest and watching me intently. I gave him a wink, which he acknowledged with a nod, and I knew he was my man.

It was my mother who contacted the ABC to suggest I might make an interesting subject for *Australian Story*. I sometimes refer to her with good-humoured irreverence as 'the unbiased mother' because she is completely prejudiced in my favour. Mum is a lioness of a woman when it comes to her only cub, and for all my thirty-four years she has been a loyal supporter, forgiving me my weaknesses and promoting my strengths as only a mother can. Knowing her ways, it came as no surprise to me to learn that her boss at Tocal Agricultural College, Cameron Archer, had suggested she write to the ABC about me. I suspect the hope was that once the goings-on of her son were addressed publicly, whenever she brought up the subject afterwards, her colleagues could simply say, 'Yes, Jennifer, we know. We saw the show.'

The proposal she submitted interested Ben Cheshire enough to set up a meeting with me. After court, I suggested we go for a drink at a café near where I live to discuss what would be involved. As the two of us crossed Hyde Park and chatted about what Ben had seen in court, I felt relaxed in his company. In the café, he endeavoured to flesh out some details to appreciate the blood and breath behind the facts of my life. I noted his impish features, his cheeky smile and expressions and warmed to him even more. His world view and sense of humour seemed very much in keeping with my own, and his questions didn't make me feel as if he was prying. Nevertheless, as I found out once the project got underway, he was determined to get to the heart of issues in order to reveal the rawness of human experience that makes a story worth telling.

Matt (forefront) with his cousin Stuart, December 1975. Stuart and Matt grew up together. When Matt was young he used to be able to walk, but the nature of his disability resulted in his paraplegia.

Through his questions, Ben also revealed a basic understanding of my significant biographical details. He knew that I was born with a rare genetic disorder, diastrophic dysplasia, resulting in my having short limbs and a spine that twisted and turned with scoliosis and kyphosis. He was aware that in 1980, at the age of ten, I had a major operation to correct this spinal problem, which resulted in paraplegia and subsequent loss of the use of my legs. He knew I'd required the use of an electric wheelchair ever since for mobility, but that these things had not prevented me attending a mainstream school in my home town of Coffs Harbour, or moving to Sydney to attain my Bachelor of Arts and Bachelor of Laws degrees.

At the end of our discussion, Ben explained that often stories never get made, and that if other, more pressing matters come up an idea can quickly be dismissed. I simply agreed that if he could convince 'the boss' I was a story worth telling, then I would participate in whatever way I could.

A few days later Ben phoned and said, 'The boss says it is a goer so let's begin.' And we did.

By good fortune, we had the luxury of months to shoot my story. I was told this was a rarity in television land, and only came about because the timetable fell within the Christmas vacation period. This meant we had time to develop a relationship and for me to become accustomed to Ben, cameraman Quentin Davis and sound recordist Scott Taylor following me around to record my daily ways and getting background on my personal history. It was an easy, conversational experience from the very beginning.

Ben and his team filmed me at work, going out to dinner, catching up with friends, attending Access Committee meetings at the City of Sydney Council, going to social functions and rugby games. There were different degrees of organisation required as we endeavoured to work as collaboratively as we could to make it happen.

Ben's approach to my story was quite simple: he wanted to encapsulate what I did in my life, reveal issues from my past and question the matters of the future. He was also in search of a turning point: the twist that would give the story a significant shift and interest. I felt I could assist with a great many details, but that the turning point would have to discover itself.

I was impressed by Ben's clever and thoughtful approach to the opening scene of my story. He wanted viewers to see and hear me in a robust environment before realising I have a profound physical disability.

He suggested that some friends and I take a trip up to the Blue Mountains. My buddy Joanne Sutton volunteered to drive my van, so we packed ourselves in and, along with one of her sisters, Dianne, and our beloved friend Gen Phillip, headed off. When we arrived, we went for a drive around some of the scenic spots. Quentin Davis attached a mini camera to the roof of the van, just

Left to right: Joanne Sutton, Michelle Morris, Matt Laffan. Joanne is Matt's friend who also featured on Australian Story. Michelle is Matt's girlfriend.

above the front passenger seat, so I could be taped as we drove along, and Scott Taylor wired us up to record our conversations. The mini camera's tight head and shoulders shots showed me chatting animatedly with my three beautiful and fabulous lady friends without any indication that I was in a wheelchair or of short stature. A few minutes later my disabilities were revealed with a shot of my complete self getting out of the van. But viewers had already been introduced to 'the true me', without being immediately distracted by my disabilities, which is a complete contrast to what happens in my everyday life.

When I told Ben I was on the New South Wales Rugby Judiciary, he was keen to get footage of one of our hearings. This required some sensitivity, because the players involved weren't expecting to discuss on national television the things they had done badly on the rugby paddock. Terry Willis, chairman of the judiciary, had to ask the consent of players and their representatives prior to the hearing in order for the filming to go ahead, and it was due to the generous spirit of all those involved that this part of the program was able to be aired. In the end, Ben used footage of a hulking rugby forward who had been sent off the field for foul play. The visual juxtaposition of the towering footballer and the judicial member of diminutive stature caused some viewers a great deal of amusement.

Ben also wanted footage of my work as a lawyer with the Office of Director of Public Prosecutions, which required more negotiation still. Cameras are not allowed into the courtroom: the anonymity of people appearing, as far as a visual record is concerned, remains important. The intrusion of a camera crew would also quickly destroy the decorum of the court proceedings, with the need to reshoot certain activities and have people repeat their statements.

I suggested Ben approach Justice Reg Blanch QC, Chief Judge of the District Court of New South Wales, to see if an alternative could be arranged. The Chief Judge was good enough to say that he would be willing to participate by providing a courtroom before the normal day's work in a mock-up situation. All we needed now was a colleague to play the part of defence counsel, and Gary Jauncy was pleased to do so.

I appear regularly in the District Court, where I conduct a list of severity appeals, all ground appeals and sentences, while also appearing regularly in the Supreme Court bails lists. I am at the coalface of the criminal legal system, dealing with a cross-section of society and society's problems, and I like to think that, more often than not, I am able to assist in the process of justice being served.

Apart from the fact that I regularly appear in front of the Chief Judge because of this role, it was personally satisfying for me to have him take part in the program because he had a major influence on the career path I took when I finished university.

Leading up to the summer of 1992–93, I was in search of a summer clerkship position prior to my last year of studies. I sought advice from a family friend, Sean Flood senior, who was with the Public Defenders at the time, to see if he could point me in the right direction. Flood introduced me to his colleague, Robert Kelleman, who suggested an arrangement at the Office of Director of Public Prosecutions (ODPP), where he had been previously employed. Kelleman made a call to his 'friend, Reg' and, before I knew it, the Director, Reg Blanch QC, was interviewing me for the position.

After my clerkship and my six months at the College of Law, I spent a further six months working for a mentions practice out of Haymarket before, midway through 1995, a lawyer's position was advertised with the ODPP. After competing in the open market for the position, I secured a role in my own right and I have not looked back since.

So it meant a great deal to me to have the Chief Judge involved in my story, as his warmth and determination to give me a start allowed me to realise my dream of working as a lawyer. Despite the fact that he had to enter the court a number of times until Quentin Davis got the perfect shot, and had to repeat his words in order for Scott Taylor's sound equipment to pick them up clearly, he remained in good humour throughout.

I quickly learned to be patient with the process of taping: the need to carry out takes and retakes can be tedious. Both Quentin and Scott are creative perfectionists and they wanted to ensure that they got the best of a situation. Whether I was meandering through city streets, riding a ferry on the harbour or simply conversing with friends, the camera and microphone became an extension of my routine and I was subconsciously aware that things had to be done right.

As a result I came to appreciate the technicalities of continuity. If I was holding a file in my hand as I entered a room, for example, I knew it was important for the next shot that I still gripped it in the same manner, even though Quentin had asked me to stop and repeat the move so he could record it from a different angle.

As the process continued it came to feel natural to be in front of the camera, to be candid and relaxed. Sometimes too relaxed.

It seems that almost every *Australian Story* episode has a barbecue scene, and mine was no exception. In order to capture a typical 'evening meal at home', Stuart Khan, my cousin and flatmate at the time, and Linda Seimon, our other flatmate, invited our friends Mandy Pearson and Joanne Sutton over for salmon steaks, pork sausages and salad. Smoke from the barbecue blew in every direction it was not supposed to, the wine was poured liberally, and Stuart, the gourmet cook, asked on camera, 'Who wants their salmon steaks well cooked and who wants them raw?'

Afterwards, fuelled by the wine we had consumed, Joanne and I began to sing (very badly) Nat King Cole's old hit 'L-O-V-E'. Scott Taylor, who always had his ear open to an opportunity, quickly got Ben's attention and suddenly we were singing the whole thing again, but even more off key.

Ben's ability to blend various scenes and examples from my daily routine with my personal history, using photographs and commentary from Mum, Dad and others, impressed me greatly. When it came to the main interview about the details of my life, and he endeavoured to reach into that private place where our fears are hidden and our dreams lurk, I found the process to be easy. It seemed we had already come to know each other, and I trusted him and his approach. He was my confidant — albeit one armed with a camera and boom microphone.

The turning point of my story presented itself to Ben during the editing process. He felt it lay in the question of whether or not I would find a partner to share my life journey.

It was Joanne Sutton — a gorgeous, flamboyant friend with whom I have shared great moments, and one of the major commentators about my life on the program — who created the pitch for this question. Her summary of me as an 'incredible flirt' was both flattering and embarrassing. Author and sports journalist Peter FitzSimons also commented on the question of my future with a partner, saying that he did not know how it would be determined, but that he hoped it would be with me finding true love. Although the program ended without the issue being resolved, it was a powerful enough sentiment to give Ben that extra bite he required.

To give colour and movement to the question, Ben latched on to a friendly date I had with one of my colleagues, Monika Knowles. Monika is a prosecuting lawyer, a very clever woman with a great deal of style and a warm heart. Around the time that the *Australian Story* crew had squeezed into my life, I'd asked Monika to see the Australian Ballet's production of *Mirror Mirror*, based on the fairytale of Sleeping Beauty. We planned to meet up after work and head down to Circular Quay for a pre-performance drink at the Oyster Bar before pushing on to the Opera House.

When Ben heard about this, he invited himself and the crew along for part of the show. So when Monika and I climbed into the back of the accessible taxi to get to Circular Quay, the crew followed us inside the cabin. Despite the intrusion of the camera and the microphone tucked into her lapel, Monika stood up to 'the date' well. She sipped her champagne, ate her oysters and conversed with me as if our evening outing was a private affair and not one that would be shared with millions of viewers.

It wasn't until the program aired that I discovered Ben had used the footage as a backdrop to the question of whether I would one day discover true love.

The day afterwards, Monika contacted me to say, 'Great show, Laffo, but I had no idea we were a romantic interest.'

I am delighted to say that, despite the television exposure, Monika and I remain good friends. As to the issue of love and finding someone to share my life — I met a marvellous woman a few years after the show was aired, and our relationship developed without a national audience watching every step.

Having been cast in a physical mould that is out of the ordinary, I am used to being recognised and was prepared for the idea that there could be some immediate fame after the show aired. However, as is the experience for many subjects of *Australian Story*, ever since the broadcast I have been spotted and greeted by people from all walks of life. It even happened in Canada, when I was leaving a hotel lobby in Vancouver: a friendly couple began the now familiar refrain, 'Excuse me, have you been on television?' Closer to home, a fellow citizen of Sydney, who happens to be homeless and lives in Hyde Park, calls out a cheerful 'Hello, Matt' every time I pass by.

My only personal regret about the program is that, due to time restraints, an important part of my life could not be included. My connection with and great affection for St John's College, a residential college at the University of Sydney, and the mates I made there, ended up on the cutting room floor. This disappointed me as my friends from that time contributed greatly to my terrific university experience, and have remained vital players in my life since. I felt the telling of my story was diminished slightly by the

Matt addressing the 'Making Connections' conference in January 2003. Matt performs regular engagements as a speaker.

absence of a decent reference to them. To this day, my college mates good-humouredly stir Ben about this omission whenever they meet him at one of my parties.

After the show I received a huge amount of mail, both of the electronic and postbox variety. Most of the writers said that the show had made them realise the potential that life held for them and how any problems they faced could be overcome. Many of the writers were school students. The scene showing me talking to the kids at Redfern Primary School must have captured the imaginations of other young Australians who watched the show. It is undeniably rewarding to know that, for whatever reason, some aspect of my story has enabled others to enhance their own lives.

However, despite the end result being such a public enterprise, the fact remains that, ultimately, the making of the program and the issues it raised were intensely personal.

The night it was shown on television, Mum, Dad and I were in different places. I was in my flat with a few friends and my cousin and flatmate. Mum was in Tocal, where she worked mid-week, nervously anticipating the revelations to be made. Dad was at the University of Sydney Football Club for rugby training, although the sessions were called off early so the players could retire to the clubhouse and watch the program with him. Despite the fact we could not watch it together, we three, as always, through the worst and best of days, were held together as a family by love.

As the story — my story — unfolded I felt overwhelmed.

In part it was because of things I hadn't known before, such as Mum's engagement ring having six diamonds to represent the number of children she and Dad had planned to have but never did. I felt fiercely protective of Mum as I watched her become emotional on screen, and I quietly urged her not to cry and to remember everything was all right.

It was also the way Ben captured the bond Dad and I share. I am enormously proud of that connection, and it was moving to see and hear it in this forum.

Then there was Ben's ability to elicit information from close friends like Nick Farr-Jones and Peter FitzSimons, and my boss

Nick Cowdery QC, and weave it together to sum up that which is my lot. And, of course, it was partly due to the way Quentin Davis had visually represented the city I love and the way I fit into it. All these reasons, and others best experienced than explained, made my *Australian Story* experience an overwhelmingly positive one

As the show ended that night, I felt exhausted and elated at the same time and I hope the program had the same effect on everyone who watched it. Judging by the letters, it did.

Left to right: John Eales, Peter FitzSimons, Nick Farr-Jones. Matt is a rugby man at heart and considers Peter FitzSimons and Nick Farr-Jones great mates and role models. Photo taken on the set of *This Is Your Life*, featuring Peter FitzSimons in 2004. Matt was one of the guests.

'While my back and eyesight hold out, I can think of no better way to earn a living.'
Cameraman Anthony Sines on location in the Kimberley.

Through the Looking Glass

Anthony Sines

Illuminated by the headlights of the four-wheel-drive,

the cabbage palms flashing past began to transform

into strange alien creatures. We were lost in the

middle of the Kimberley, but in denial. Each of us was

convinced the turn-off to the camp was somewhere

different and by now we'd been driving for hours over

bone-jarring, teeth-rattling corrugated dirt roads.

Fatigue was taking its toll.

Marc Smith, the sound recordist in our small production team (think Hagrid without the beard), was perhaps suffering the most. His head was making infrequent but considerable contact with the roof of the bush-basher, while the rumbling of his stomach was almost overwhelming the drone of the diesel engine. Frustration and anger vibrated from his side of the cabin as his blood sugar level dropped, and I knew the time for indecision was running out.

In the back, the producer of the story we were working on was worried — with some justification. In this wild and remote location, Rebecca Latham was relying on two clueless city boys to see her home safely. Her sighs of exasperation were replaced with groans of annoyance. With fear dawned clarity.

'The sat phone — use the bloody sat phone, will you!' she suggested.

Marc and I exchanged glances, and I reached for the mobile lifeline with studied indifference. There's an unwritten rule among crews that prohibits us from acknowledging that a producer or journalist may have something to contribute. But needs must, and the reassuring sound of the dial tone did drown out the rumbling emanating from Marc's direction for a few minutes.

If only Burke and Wills had had the luxury of a line of communication from the heart of the desert into space and back again. Our local guide talked us past the endless rows of cabbage palms back to camp, but not to bed. There were still batteries to charge, lenses to dust and tapes to sort. Documentary-making is that sort of job: the extraordinary and the mundane in constant competition.

On this day, the extraordinary had won out. We'd flown to a secret location to film a remarkable man called Grahame Walsh who had rediscovered some truly mind-blowing 27,000-year-old rock art.

As I finally fell asleep in the early hours of the morning, strange images of the Wandjinas — eerie spaceman-like figures, more recent than the Bradshaw paintings with which they shared the cliffs — made their way off the rock face and into my exhausted slumber. Bulbous heads bobbed in and out of waves of spinifex or cooled themselves in the black waterholes of the Mitchell Plateau.

I woke, dazed, just after 6 am and sought out my similarly tousled and taciturn team members. Marc never truly wakes up until he's managed to stuff a loaf of bread into the toaster and then himself.

We had been in the Kimberley only a few days. Most of that time had been spent well off the beaten track, trying to catch up with Grahame who was taking some wealthy, elderly Melburnian women on a tour of his favourite sites. I couldn't help thinking that the ability of these matriarchs to keep up the pace was a story in itself, but Rebecca was more interested in capturing Grahame enthusing over some particularly fine examples of the Bradshaw art.

Like so many of the fascinating people I'm fortunate to meet shooting *Australian Story*, Grahame Walsh is at the eye of a storm. This intellectually gifted man with little formal education has become the world expert on the Bradshaws — beautiful and delicately painted pictures so named because they were 'discovered' by Joseph Bradshaw in 1891. But it is Grahame who has been responsible for locating most of them and meticulously cataloguing them over many years.

The origin of the paintings is mysterious, and they generate considerable controversy because they appear older and quite different from other forms of Aboriginal art. They have become Grahame's magnificent obsession — and the stocky, fifty-something former service-station owner is harder to keep up with than the Energizer bunny.

Today would involve another long drive following sketchy directions — a daunting prospect given that my wife always says I could get lost in a supermarket.

After piling bubble wrap, sponge and any other padding I could find into the back of the four-wheel-drive, we loaded the camera gear and headed off in search of our elusive quarry. Staying close to the 'talent' (as we call the people who inhabit our stories) without getting too close is a delicate balancing act. Most people don't know what they're taking on when they agree to allow us into their lives, and the gruelling duration of the shoot can fray even the strongest nerves. In short, it is possible to have too much of even us and more than one person has been known to resort to quite colourful language in an effort to get us to bugger off. Marc, especially, has been privileged to overhear some quite interesting assessments of the filming process from people who have forgotten they're wearing a radio mike capable of transmitting over a considerable distance.

Grahame was proving particularly evasive. As we rattled along, Marc and I passed the time chatting about our current obsession: mountain biking. Rebecca, who had been tortured by slight variations of the same conversation over several days, threatened to kill us both and let the dingoes pick over our remains. Fortunately, a strange yellow shape wavering through the heat haze changed the mood.

As it loomed closer we realised it was that most ubiquitous of off-road vehicles, the kombi van. This one was loaded to the gunnels with tourists. As we passed I smiled and said hello and they answered in their excellent Scandinavian English. Mad Swedes in the middle of the Kimberley, I thought. What could they possibly be doing here? Grahame told me later that they were there to see the Bradshaws. They and many like them share experiences and the GPS coordinates of the vulnerable artworks on the internet. Soon, nowhere on earth will be beyond the reach of adventurous tourists and no natural or cultural wonder truly secret or protected.

Finally we saw the rocky outcrop that was our landmark. We drove as close as we could, then set out on foot. It was hot — in the high thirties. In the distance we could see Grahame's vehicles. How did he get further in than us, we grumbled as we tried to find a track across some swampy ground.

Walking through some knee-length grass I heard rustling. A snake? But no, the naked buttocks before me were all too human. With a wave of embarrassment I realised I'd walked into the camp's toilet area. Fortunately, I was too concerned with where to put my feet to make eye contact with the elderly lady hurriedly pulling up her jodhpurs. Seeing people at their most exposed is nothing new on *Australian Story*, but it's usually in an emotional sense rather than a literal one.

When I finally arrived at the camp, it was to find Grahame fiddling with his still camera and lenses and enthusing over the types of paintings we'd be seeing. This would be 'catch as catch can' filming. The irrepressible Grahame wasn't the sort to wait while shots, scenes and sequences were set up for our convenience. Marc stomped his own path through the bush, just in time to set off again in pursuit of cultural treasure.

I had to think on my feet while trying to avoid losing my step as we clambered up rock faces and slipped on loose gravel. Rebecca was whispering to me her thoughts on what might happen next, but reality has a tendency to be unpredictable. Around one corner we came across signs that past visitors had worshipped at the base of some of the paintings. Unfortunately, the candle remnants and related smoke had damaged the very artworks they came to praise. Grahame was despondent but he understands better than anyone the attraction of the Bradshaws.

It was now my turn to answer the call of nature and, wary of the earlier incident, I travelled some distance in search of privacy. I looked up to see a magnificent panel of elegant action figures, as Grahame describes them: ancient paintings of men with elongated heads hunting with spears. I mentioned them to Grahame when I returned and he said he hadn't seen that panel before. We went back to photograph them and, for the first time perhaps, I began to understand the joy of discovery and what drove Grahame to spend so much of his life so far from what most of us regard as civilisation. Unfortunately, none of this was on film and I wasn't part of the story, so Rebecca was underwhelmed by my epiphany. The journalistic curse of the deadline was haunting her.

After eight rolls of digital betacam tape, and with remaining batteries fading fast, we decided to call it a day. We were all spent, and the dust on the front of the lens was starting to give Grahame an unwelcome, if flattering Hollywood glow. Not to mention the fact that the gear was still working after several days of dust, vibration and heat — you have to know when not to push your luck.

I am always impressed by the reliability of our equipment, considering all the tiny plastic bits and pieces and delicate little circuits inside. I've never yet lost a camera (touch wood), although colleagues have been forced to file paperwork listing such reasons for the loss of their gear as 'taken by a crocodile' and 'forgot to shut the tailgate of the crew car'. To his credit, on this Kimberley trip Marc almost eclipsed all those legendary achievements by nearly causing a chopper crash when his headphones flew off during a flight and were caught by the cord just short of the tail rotor. Thank goodness he was too heavy to fly with me.

However, one shouldn't be too smug. Once, on another chopper ride over Kakadu, I almost came a cropper by leaning out with my camera as the aircraft banked to get that special shot. I thought I was wearing a safety harness but it turned out someone had forgotten to attach it to its anchor. It would have been more than just the camera that was taken had I fallen into those waters.

The thing is, in this job you never know what's around the corner — something that was driven home to all of us the next day.

We'd been up early to film some sunrise shots not far from the former cattle property where we were staying. After a little exploring with Grahame, we returned home for a welcome lunch and the obligatory cups of tea in the afternoon heat. Marc, Rebecca and I were sitting under a tree chatting (a surprising thing in itself because, after a few days of living in close quarters, sometimes things can get a little strained) when a convoy of vehicles arrived. Policemen and Aboriginal locals got out and it soon became apparent this was no courtesy call.

We picked up the gear and filmed as they searched Grahame's camp. The looks on their faces told us we were the last people they expected to see. We felt the same way about them. Rebecca, in a burst of inner-city Sydney paranoia, told me to hide the tapes in case the police confiscated them. Not that easy to do at short notice: by this stage there was half a suitcase full of them. In any case, although the police took our names and details, we weren't part of the main game. They'd flown in to check that no artefacts had been removed from the locations Grahame had been cataloguing. They found nothing and, after a brief talk with Grahame, left as quickly as they'd arrived.

From our perspective the raid was a gift: we now had another dramatic incident to weave into the story. But it also highlighted the different approach of the Sydney producers and the Brisbane crew, Marc and me. To them, we must have appeared annoyingly laidback, unconcerned and, dare I say it, even a little lazy perhaps. To us, they often seem over-anxious, pedantic and stressed out.

Sometimes the culture clash is just plain funny. One eccentric producer from Sydney we're particularly fond of working with once grabbed the microphone as we were rolling on a useful bit of sound. 'Roll on this, roll on this,' he instructed, making it all completely useless. In the same way, a producer might destroy good vision by shaking my arm as I'm filming in order to ensure I am filming and not just looking through the lens for my own entertainment. Still, I in turn have been known to nod off during lengthy interviews, more than once waking to discover the talent has moved completely out of frame or that the tape has run out. Similarly, I've detected what sounded suspiciously like snoring coming from Marc's direction. Either that or a grizzly bear in hibernation had made its way into the room. In our defence, though, these rare incidents have usually occurred sometime after midnight and well into a fifteen-hour day.

In all seriousness, *Australian Story* interviews, while often not as physically demanding as the Grahame Walsh shoot, can certainly be emotionally harrowing. The experiences that the featured individuals and their families share are often heartbreaking. Yet the chance to listen, unedited, to what some of these remarkable people have to say is a wonderful and inspirational privilege. It's impossible to be unmoved by the story of Sam Bailey, for example, who became a quadriplegic at the age of nineteen, but refused to give up on his dream of running his own farm; or the candid recollections of a cancer survivor, Danielle Tindle, who appeared positively serene while recounting the challenge of overcoming relentless bad news, complete physical breakdown and unimaginable pain on her long road to recovery; or to hear surgeon Michael Holt talk about his determination to continue in his profession after he was knocked down by a car and left partially blind. And, from my point of view, the best thing about the Wayne Bennett story was not seeing him behind the scenes with the Broncos; it was watching him interact with his family. Here was a man who knew what was really important in life. I think that explains the ongoing popularity of the program: there is something in these stories for all of us.

And sometimes we meet interesting people during the course of a shoot who never make it onto the small screen. I can think of a case in point on the Grahame Walsh story. The caretaker couple we stayed with on the former cattle station were a classic country pair, hospitable and down to earth. During the evening meal of recently butchered feral beef and stewed rhubarb, carefully prepared by our hostess, it was clear that our host was champing at the bit to get through dinner. We wondered why he was being so impatient.

While his wife was clearing the table, he took us into the lounge room where an unusual shape crouched hunched under a sheet. With a gleam in his eye and a hand movement a world-class magician would have been proud of, our host swept the linen aside to reveal a brand new, absolutely immaculate Harley-Davidson motorcycle. It had just forty kilometres on the clock and we could have eaten dinner off the saddle and licked dessert from the front tyre.

I thought it was an unusual place to keep such a fine piece of automotive engineering and asked where he intended to ride it. 'Oh, I wouldn't ride it outside,' he said horrified. 'Too much gravel and too much bull dust.'

'But then why is it all the way out here?' we asked.

With a wink and a nimbleness a much younger man would have found hard to emulate, our host hopped on the back of the beast and she roared into life. And I do mean roared. Over the top of the racket, he shouted, 'It's me and me wife's retirement present. We'll go right round Australia one day soon.'

The noise subsided but his dream continued to reverberate around the homestead. How lucky are we, I thought, that our jobs allow us to see so much of this country and meet so many diverse and wonderful people.

On the long flight from Kununurra back to Brisbane I thought over the events of the past few days. It'd been one of those shoots that had just about everything. From my point of view, the only thing missing was a re-enactment — the dramatisations *Australian Story* uses to illustrate past events and emotions. Creatively these can be lots of fun and very challenging. Sometimes they are mini-film shoots as we struggle to give a stylistic impression of the subject's experience. Sometimes they are like magic tricks, smoke and mirrors held together with pieces of wire and clever editing. A plane crash can be recreated using a ceiling fan and an old fridge door. A violent encounter can be re-enacted with film noir grit using high-key lighting and blurred shots of gravel filmed in the ABC car park after midnight. But, like all the best magic, it only works if the audience is prepared to suspend disbelief and doesn't look too closely, so I'll say no more.

People of many ages and all walks of life watch and enjoy *Australian Story*, and they're always keen to hear about life behind the lens. While I may never be rich, I meet people who are. While I may never be inspirational (except hopefully to my kids), I know what it is to be inspired. And, while my back and eyesight hold out, I can think of no better way to earn a living.

While Aaron McMillan underwent marathon surgery, his family prayed at a makeshift shrine to Aaron in the hospital room where he had practised piano.

Playing for Time

Ben Cheshire

In 2001, pianist Aaron McMillan was diagnosed with a brain tumour so large that there was a risk that it would kill him within six weeks. Producer Ben Cheshire heard about the diagnosis a few days later, and arranged to follow Aaron, as doctors decided how best to treat the twenty-four-year-old musician.

For the *Australian Story* crew it was a dramatic week, culminating in a marathon operation to attempt to remove the tumour.

For eight tense hours, we'd been inside an operating theatre at Prince of Wales Hospital. As the camera rolled, two neurosurgeons worked non-stop to try to save the life of the man on the operating table. It was uncomfortably cold in there, the temperature lowered to reduce the risk of infection. Finally, one of the surgeons emerged to say a few words. It was not good.

'Things are looking pretty grim,' the surgeon said. 'The patient's brain has swollen, making it more difficult to get at the tumour inside.'

Word had been sent to the family to prepare for possible bad news.

From a phone in a tiny side room, I called the executive producer of *Australian Story*, Deb Fleming. Though I had only known Aaron a few days, it was hard to get the words out because of the lump in my throat. 'There may not be a happy ending with this one,' I stumbled. All we could do was watch and wait.

It was a dramatic moment in what turned out to be the most intense week of my career. We often interview people about events that have changed their lives. But it was unusual to be there with them as the moment unfolded. This time we were on a roller-coaster ride together, and nobody knew how it would end.

Five days earlier, my weekend had been interrupted by a phone call from a friend, Belinda Caldwell, telling me about the young pianist who had just been diagnosed with a brain tumour 'as big as a cricket ball'. Belinda's mother had been one of Aaron McMillan's teachers at the Glenaeon Rudolf Steiner School in Sydney. She and some of Aaron's other friends had visited him in hospital the night before and watched him entertain the nurses and guests on an electric piano that had been set up in an empty ward. Driving home afterwards, they were shocked by the possibility that this talented man could be dead in six weeks. Wouldn't it be good, they thought, if somebody could take some film of Aaron before it was too late? Hence the phone call the next morning from Belinda, who knew I worked on *Australian Story*.

As luck would have it, I was looking for a new story idea. So

I jumped in the car and drove to the hospital, where I found Aaron sitting up in bed and happy to chat. I listened as he told me how his life had been turned upside down by a casual visit to the doctor twelve days before. He'd noticed what he thought was a minor infection in one eye. His local GP, Dr Barbara Schiff, had given him some medication, but when the infection hadn't cleared up a week later she seemed concerned. She tested his peripheral vision and kept asking questions. Had he been experiencing headaches? Had he vomited recently? Was anything else troubling him?

Ninety minutes later he found himself in a city clinic undergoing a CAT scan. Three hours after that Dr Schiff phoned and asked him to come back to her surgery. The scan had revealed something and it was 'pretty bad', she said. Taking his grandparents along for some moral support, Aaron was told he had one of the biggest brain tumours ever found in a living person. It had probably been growing in his head for ten years and, if left untreated, could cause a seizure and death within six weeks.

For someone who'd just been given that sort of news, Aaron seemed reasonably calm. I told him about the kind of programs made by *Australian Story*, and asked how he would feel about having a camera follow his progress over the next few days. Somewhat to my surprise, he said yes.

Some time later, Aaron explained his decision to me.

Aaron speaks to the crew from *Australian Story*, just before his operation.

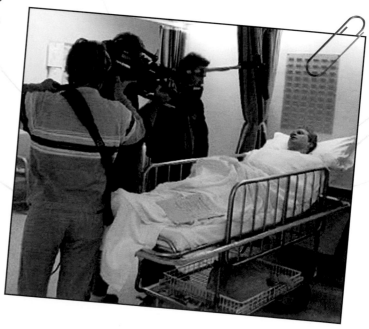

When I was diagnosed with the brain tumour, I really wasn't very sure that I was going to get through it. A lot of the news we were being told by the surgeon was pretty devastatingly bad. I was sort of talked into the filming by those friends who said that if the worst case scenario did eventuate, there would be an interesting record of what did happen. And if there was any potential for it to be a really positive story, that would be a good way of contributing the experience for people to use as a comfort or role model for getting through these types of things.

The next thing was to seek the permission of Prince of Wales Hospital. From the hospital lobby I rang their public affairs manager, Charles Maddison, who offered no objection, provided we respected the privacy of other patients. *Australian Story*'s Sydney film crew was away on another shoot, so I contacted a terrific freelancer, Steve Hider, and asked whether he was free for a couple of days. We arranged to begin filming the following day, with sound recordist Teigan Kollosche. There wasn't a moment to lose.

Neurosurgeon Dr Charlie Teo was to attempt the removal of the tumour. But, as it turned out, our first shoot wasn't at the hospital; it was at the practice nets of Sydney Cricket Ground. In an interesting sideline from his music, Aaron was coach and mentor to a young cricketer, Elliot Bullock. He slipped out of hospital to have a hit with Elliot, perhaps for the last time.

Later that afternoon, in a hospital ward that was empty and awaiting renovation, we recorded the key interview with Aaron. Though barely an hour long — much shorter than usual — it provided the narration for most of the program. Aaron was already proving to be what's known in the industry as 'good talent': able to articulate his story with intelligence, humour and emotion.

Film crew wearing hospital scrubs pose with Aaron's friends and family.

Over the next few days we met a colourful cast of characters as Aaron's friends and family dropped in to visit. David Wansbrough, a poet, playwright and priest, came bearing an original Chagall painting. Former Test cricketer Gavin Robertson turned up with a promise to continue the mentoring of young Elliot if something happened to Aaron. INXS guitarist Tim Farris, wearing a white Stetson, came up with a nickname for Dr Teo: 'Chucky T'. Aaron gave piano lessons to a neighbour, Steve Leong, and found time for a session with his own teacher, the legendary Neta Maughan. Aaron's mother, Gale Puckett, told us how Aaron had loved the piano from the moment he started playing at age nine and had written his first composition before he was ten. Artist Peter Crisp tried to liaise between Aaron and the visitors, but there were so many that Charles Maddison — an unusually cooperative hospital public relations manager — had to formally counsel Aaron to quieten things down.

Most likely, Aaron was keeping his mind busy to avoid dwelling on the awful possibility that he could be dead in a matter of days. Dr Teo had said there was a five to ten per cent chance of him dying on the operating table.

'It is quite extraordinary that he continues to play the piano well,' Dr Teo told us. 'The tumour is in the area of the brain that controls vision and artistic expression — all the things you would think are absolutely necessary to play the piano. Given its location, size and the amount of swelling, I am not looking forward to removing that tumour. I'm finding it very daunting. I hope that everything would turn out well, but I am very scared that they might not.'

At 7 am on day four of the shoot, we got to the hospital to find Aaron restless and pacing the room. He'd been up late the night before, recording a similarly restless piece of music by the Greek composer Xenakis, to 'get himself in the mood for surgery'. That music became the soundtrack for the next part of our story.

Aaron gathered his belongings for a temporary shift to Royal Prince Alfred Hospital. There the doctors hoped to embolise the tumour — cut off its blood supply, causing it to shrink and bleed less during the forthcoming operation. But first they had to perform an angiogram to determine whether the vessels carrying blood to the tumour were also supplying blood to the brain. If that was the case, there was nothing they could do.

Aaron was strapped into the machine and a needle was inserted into his groin. A fine plastic catheter was fed through his body to the blood vessels in his neck.

Neuroradiologist Dr Geoffrey Parker was watching the progress on a monitor. He grimaced. 'It's not worth doing anything with that,' he muttered. Unfortunately, the angiogram showed there were no vessels that carried blood exclusively to the tumour. Embolisation of the tumour was impossible without cutting off the blood supply to Aaron's brain.

Dr Parker phoned Dr Teo. The two specialists agreed that the operation would be a challenge. It was brought forward to the following day.

An ambulance took Aaron back to Prince of Wales Hospital. We filmed him lying prone inside. Aaron was determined to maintain a positive outlook, but I wondered what was really going on inside his mind.

That night Aaron had a last chat with his mother and with Charlie Teo. He shook hands with Dr Teo and kissed his mother goodbye.

Then he motioned me over to the bed. There was something he wanted to say, not for the camera, just for the microphone.

Just as a game, tell yourself that you could be six weeks from the end of your life. Right now. You could be! Suddenly a lot of complicated things become very simple. You can forget about all the things that revolve around you, and start focusing on the reason you were given this life in the first place. Find what it is that binds you to this life, because we're given the opportunity to work on that every single day. And then one day, suddenly, it can all be taken away.

Those words became the opening lines of the program, over shots of Aaron at the piano.

We were back at the hospital at six thirty the following morning. Everything seemed slightly surreal as Aaron was wheeled into the operating theatre and the anaesthetist unwrapped his vials of drugs. I wanted to say something to Aaron, but what do you say to someone who is facing a life or death moment?

'Whatever happens, you're a hell of a piano player,' was the best I could muster.

Then Aaron was under, the anaesthetist getting no reply to his question, 'Are you still with us, mate?'

It was to be a marathon operation and Charlie Teo had come prepared with a stack of CDs to keep himself alert and motivated. The sounds of John Denver and Abba drifted through the operating theatre as the hours passed. Dr Teo peered into what looked like a submarine periscope while his gloved hands meticulously removed tiny particles of tumour, one after another. To his side, a TV screen showed everything in gory close-up.

Upstairs, Aaron's family and friends were in a waiting room, listening to one of his piano CDs. Aaron's mother, who hadn't struck me as a particularly religious woman, was praying aloud for a happy outcome. The surgeons had warned that Aaron might survive the operation but be unable to speak or play music. Aaron had told us he wanted to survive with his senses intact, or not survive at all.

It was mid-afternoon when word was sent to the family to prepare for possible bad news. The family were restricted to the waiting room but the film crew had complete access to the surgeons, so I became the unofficial messenger between the two.

Had I heard anything more? What did I make of the warning they had just been given, asked Aaron's mum.

I broached the awkward subject of what we would do in the event of Aaron dying on the operating table. Should we give the family a few moments alone before barging in with our TV camera? Gail and I decided on a kind of secret signal: if they could see the camera when the doctors came to talk to them at the end of the operation, it would mean good news. If there was no camera, it signalled bad news — and we would leave them alone for a while.

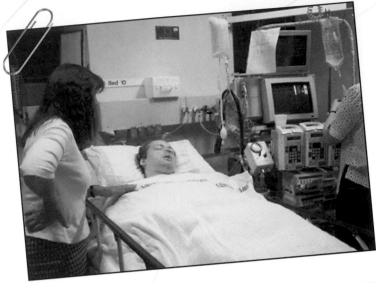

Aaron's mother, Gail Puckett, spends a few moments with her son after the operation. 'He looks like he's done ten rounds with Muhammad Ali.'

Darkness fell. Aaron's family and friends meditated by candle-light while Charlie Teo kept scraping away at the tumour.

'At times like this, you can't give up, you just keep at it,' he said. Twelve hours had passed since the operation began and Charlie had yet to take a moment's break.

After another hour or so I noticed a change of mood in the operating room. The medicos seemed to be packing up. In front of me, one nurse was cleaning what looked like a ceramic bowl. With a shudder I realised it was the top of Aaron's skull, about to be glued back in place. It struck me that the human body is a lot like a Meccano set, with bits that can be unscrewed, fixed up and put back again.

The anaesthetist woke Aaron up, asked him to wiggle his toes and squeeze his hands. From the smiles all around, it was obvious the operation had been a success.

Dr Teo asked me to fetch the family from upstairs, and there were squeals of delight as he told them that all the tumour had been removed. Gail spent a few minutes alone with Aaron before inviting everyone for a celebratory glass of wine. We all felt as if we had witnessed a miracle, creating a strange kind of bond between us that would last forever.

As I drove home at about 1 am, I almost knocked down a care-less cyclist who ran a red light and had no helmet or bike lights. I felt like getting out and yelling at him, 'Don't you know how precious life is? I just saw a man's life being saved, and you want to throw yours away?' But he had darted away into the night.

The next morning we interviewed Dr Schiff, the GP whom Charlie Teo credited with really saving Aaron's life. Then it was back to the hospital to see Aaron.

He was typically upbeat, though with his swollen face he looked like he'd gone ten rounds with the boxer Mohammed Ali. Unfortunately, we had just missed a magic moment when he climbed out of bed to play the piano for Dr Teo, who had brought his children along for the visit. But we knew we had a great story, and Aaron was already talking about something that would make a wonderful ending.

Just four weeks later, Aaron McMillan gave a triumphant concert at the Yass property of artist Peter Crisp, accompanied by the Canberra Youth Orchestra. The audience was full of faces we had met at the hospital. They danced into the night, and straggled in for a sumptuous country breakfast the following morning. We left to complete the editing of the story, which was to air the following week.

There was a last-minute panic on broadcast day over a swear word in the program. Unorthodox cleric David Wansbrough had been tired and emotional when we interviewed him during a visit to the hospital not long after Aaron's tumour was diagnosed. 'He just can't bloody die,' said Wansbrough. 'I'm a clergyman, but fuck the cosmos, you just feel angry that somebody with all these gifts, who looks better than all of us, has to face this.'

The program was sent to the ABC's censor for a decision on whether the offending word had to be removed. I argued against its removal: it was the fact that the comment was made by a clergyman that gave it such a powerful impact. It was decided that an announcement would be made at the beginning of the program, warning that it contained offensive language.

When 'Playing for Time' was broadcast, viewers responded in droves to the positive outlook maintained by Aaron throughout his ordeal. This was exactly what he had hoped for.

> It turned out that it became a great source of inspiration for many people, and I was proud to be a part of that. What I also found was that having the whole process filmed gave me a very interesting focal point. I was able to focus on the direction that my

story was heading. And the fact that I was not just battling through this on my own, but I was taking people on a journey — which is kind of what I do on stage as a musician — I found a great source of comfort. It was a reassuring thing, that I was sharing the story and creating a focus on getting through it, rather than just sitting there and trying to fight it on my own.

Aaron continued to have periodic brain scans, but there was no sign of the tumour returning. In 2003, he became the youngest performer to play solo at the Sydney Opera House, also putting out a CD of the concert. In the same year we made an *Australian Story* program on the larger-than-life Dr Charlie Teo, who had struck up a lasting friendship with Aaron. Aaron was a star of a benefit concert for the Cure For Life Foundation, set up by Dr Teo to fund research into brain tumours.

Then, at the beginning of 2004, came a bombshell. Steve Leong, Aaron's friend, neighbour and piano student, phoned me to say Aaron was back in hospital. New tumours had been discovered, this time in his bones. I pointed the car towards Prince of Wales Hospital with a heavy heart. Surely it couldn't be happening all over again?

Aaron lay back in his hospital bed and told me what had happened. Five months before, he had developed a stiff jaw, which he'd blamed on his habit of clenching his teeth while practising the piano. The dentist suggested he see a chiropractor.

On the morning after the second treatment, it felt as if his neck had just collapsed. He was in absolute agony, so bad he had to be taken to hospital on a stretcher. But various X-rays and scans could find nothing wrong. Eventually, the pain lessened to the point where he could walk, but the soreness in his neck never went away completely.

More recently, Aaron had seen a different doctor, who was alarmed that the pain was still there after nearly five months. He booked Aaron in that day for a different type of magnetic scanning. Within hours, Charlie Teo was on the phone, wanting to see the scans right away.

Aaron said at that point his heart really sank:

Because I thought, oh god, here we go again. As soon as you put Charlie Teo in the picture, instantly all the alarm bells start ringing again. And so I took those scans over to his office, and he sat there looking through hundreds of images. And then he suddenly just swore and said, 'Yeah, it looks like a tumour.'

And Dr Teo said to me, very disturbingly, 'I've got to go and find out whether anyone has survived a recurrence of this type.' And that was a pretty stressful thing to hear.

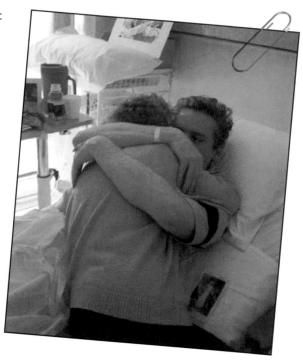

Aaron hugs his grandmother before surgery.

Further scans had revealed a total of five tumours: one in the neck, one in a rib, two in his spine, and one in his hip. The doctors suspected that malignant tumour cells may have been in Aaron's body for years, perhaps since birth, and were now starting to multiply and grow into full tumours. Because there were so many of them, and because of the awkward location of the tumour in his neck, surgery wasn't an option. Radiotherapy looked like the best possible treatment, with priority going to the tumour in the neck that could spread to the spinal cord.

Aaron and I looked at each other, both feeling rather helpless.

'Well, this was really a social visit,' I said. 'But I suppose the question has to be asked: how would you feel about having a film crew follow you around again?'

Once again, Aaron said yes. As before, he wanted to demonstrate the power of thinking positive.

This time around, I don't want to leave a remembrance video, but I'm using that idea of taking people on a journey with me and showing them what's possible. I really feel as though this as a process helps me to nail down my direction and plan things well, make things understandable to people. And I feel as though it's not just me on my own, but I'm sharing this experience with people as a benefit to everybody.

A few weeks later, we filmed Aaron's twenty-seventh birthday party with 150 people on board a Sydney harbour cruise boat. He seemed determined to make a big splash of it; perhaps, I wondered, because it might be his last.

His radiotherapist, Dr Robert Smee, had outlined a worst case scenario: if the tumour in his neck spread to the spinal cord, he could be dead within twelve weeks. Aaron had asked a direct question: was he likely to be still alive in five years? The answer was no.

Charlie Teo, who was at the birthday party, disagreed, telling us he had read about a patient who had survived the same type of tumours for twenty-six years. But Charlie still felt as though he had let Aaron down somehow.

In March 2004, Aaron was visiting his family in Brisbane when he collapsed. He'd suffered a seizure and was close to death. But his mother heard his shouts for help and called the paramedics, who gave her directions by phone on how to keep Aaron's airway free until the ambulance arrived.

It was a rude shock, not just for Aaron but for those of us who'd hoped it would be some time before his condition worscned. By coincidence *Australian Story* had arranged to record Aaron that weekend with one of his pet projects, a schoolboy rock band called Indicator. With Aaron now in Royal Brisbane Hospital, there had to be a change of plan. Instead of filming him with the band, we filmed the band rehearsing and then played the tapes to Aaron in hospital as the boys crowded around his bed. Then we filmed that too.

Back in Sydney a few weeks later, it seemed the crisis had passed. Aaron resumed his regular radiotherapy sessions at Prince of Wales Hospital. A face cast held his head tightly in place as laser beams silently attacked the tumours in his neck. The beams could be dangerous, so we had to focus the camera, press the record button and then leave the room while Aaron was being treated.

Despite feeling tired and looking a little lopsided because of the discomfort in his neck, Aaron turned up for a prior concert booking in the small town of Jamberoo. Swallowing painkillers and warning the audience that he was feeling a little light-headed, he went on to give a courageous performance, pausing to chat with the audience about why he had chosen each piece. Watching from the side, I felt moved as Aaron responded to the standing ovation given him.

'Recently I was told I may have only twelve weeks to live,' he said to the crowd. 'Well, that was thirteen weeks ago.'

When the time came for the 2004 Cure For Life benefit concert, we had the opportunity to give something back to Aaron in thanks for all the cooperation and open access he had given us. Taking the footage we had recorded of him with members of Indicator, we put together a video clip that became a highlight of the evening.

Despite his health problems, Aaron still had big plans for his music career. In October that year, our cameras recorded his second concert at the Sydney Opera House. It was the first time anyone had performed a solo piano recital at the Opera House with a repertoire of entirely Australian compositions.

At the time of writing, new tumours had just been found in Aaron's body, bringing the total to nine. Worryingly, for the first time one of them was in his soft tissue, not his bones. On my desk, the file marked 'Aaron McMillan Revisited' remains open but incomplete. The project continues, but, once again, no one knows how this story will end.

I asked Aaron what he would like done with the material if he was not around to see it.

'Well, I'm happy for this film to be used in whatever way is beneficial. But I'm not really considering that too much as a prospect. I'm fully intending to still be here, fighting, long after you guys have given up following me around.'

Chris Ferguson at the Jensen shooting trial at the Supreme Court, Victoria.

In the Line of Duty

Brigid Donovan

Sometimes it's the stories behind the stories — the

things people are reluctant to talk about — that make

the most compelling television. When we started

filming Inspector Chris Ferguson for the *Australian*

Story episode 'In the Line of Duty', we had no idea

the program would end up as an exclusive insight

into a controversial murder trial that had happened

a decade before.

In 1998, trainee producer Jacqueline Arias read a newspaper article about road accident trauma and the work of the Accident Investigation Section of the Victorian Police, led by Inspector Chris Ferguson. The unit investigated road fatalities, where there was often criminal negligence on the part of the surviving driver, and was the only one of its kind in the country. Jacqueline made the initial contact with Chris Ferguson, believing he could make an interesting subject for *Australian Story*.

When Jacqueline spoke with Chris, she was impressed by his ability to avoid getting bogged down in police jargon. There is no reporter voice-over in *Australian Story*; we rely heavily on the ability of the subjects to tell their own stories. We had no doubt that Chris Ferguson would be a fascinating and articulate storyteller; it was just a matter of how much he was prepared to talk about.

We followed Inspector Ferguson and his team of accident investigators over a two-week period. We had terrific access as Chris had briefed his investigators to call us as soon as a road trauma report came in. The AIS's brief was to attend fatal road crashes where specialist investigation skills were required in the likelihood of someone being charged over the collision: for example, where three or more people had died; or where police were involved in the crash, such as a police pursuit.

'A lot of the people that we see in road fatalities, that's the last thing that would go through their mind is to get in that car and want to kill someone,' Chris explained. 'But unfortunately for a lot of them, it's the biggest mistake they have ever made. Probably they've lived a blameless life, but I always look at it from the point of view that you're just as dead being killed by a motor car than if you are with a gun.'

I thought I'd left my days of reporting on 'fatals' long behind. Visiting a crash scene is something you never forget and I had been to dozens during my time as a newspaper police rounds reporter. We had arranged with Chris to be on twenty-four-hour call, aware that tragedy often strikes at uncivilised hours. It was an uncomfortable feeling waiting for the phone to ring with news that would give us our footage while devastating the lives of many forever.

I was at lunch with friends, celebrating my birthday, when the call came from Chris. 'It's the big one,' he said. A two-car head-on collision on a country road had left three people dead and an eight-year-old girl in hospital. The girl had lost her mother, who had been driving one car. The other two deaths were a couple in the other car.

As cameraman Patrick Stone, sound recordist Tony Helos and I drove to Rosedale, Gippsland, I couldn't help thinking about the fragility of life. As Chris had said, 'You tend to think about your life immediately prior to the incident and how quickly it can happen.'

We felt apprehensive as we approached the taped-off scene. It was illuminated by a massive flame, erected by the State Emergency Service. The three bodies were still in their smashed cars and an eerie silence enveloped the scene. Then the mechanical 'jaws of life' went into action.

Chris and his team were very sensitive to our reactions to the situation and explained the investigative process in detail. Nevertheless, it was a slow and cautious drive home that night.

Chris Ferguson dealt with death every day as head of the AIS. He explained how he coped with such tragic scenes.

> When you are dealing with people and grief and you are seeing carnage all the time, you have got to move beyond that and it becomes an investigation. If you can come to a conclusion and find out why this collision occurred and someone died, that's going to help the relatives understand and help them come to terms with their grief.

'I think it's fortunate that after twenty years in the force, he is still able to personalise death,' Chris's wife, Trish, told us. 'I'd hate him to come home and be a robot going to those scenes and saying it's just another dead body, another day at the office. When Chris comes home from an accident he feels the need to tell me what's happened … his way of debriefing, I guess, is to explain to me the human elements of the things he's seen, not to tell me all the gory things.' This was shaping up to be a fascinating story in itself, but as we got to know Chris and his family better, he revealed that there was a great deal more to his life than his recent work with the accident squad.

In 1993, Chris Ferguson was one of eight police officers charged with the murder of a suspected armed robber, Graeme Jensen, in controversial circumstances in 1988. Unfortunately for Chris, it was his first day on the job with the Armed Robbery Squad and, although he was present at the shooting, he never fired his gun.

Although the charges were eventually dropped in 1995, the eight officers had already suffered the humiliation and trauma of being charged with murder and having their police badges taken from them. I was a newspaper police reporter at the time, and it was obviously a huge story, so I recognised the significance of what Chris was telling us.

None of the charged police officers had ever spoken publicly about their ordeal; in fact, there was an unofficial agreement between them not to speak to the media. The situation was particularly sensitive because the officer who investigated the Jensen shooting for the homicide squad — and was also Chris Ferguson's mentor — was charged with accessory after the fact to murder (and suicided before the charges against him were eventually dropped).

It had all the makings of a great story — apart from one problem. Chris didn't want to talk about it on camera.

As the shoot progressed, we found that any time the cameras weren't rolling, Chris would end up talking about the traumatic experience of being charged and how it had affected his family. Chris's father had a stroke and his mother had a heart attack during the time he was suspended, possibly as a result of the stress of the whole situation. Nevertheless, Chris believed the experience had made him a better police officer.

> Having been a policeman for this length of time, I know what grief is like. I've been through grief myself and there is a saying, walk a

mile in my shoes and you'll understand how I feel. Well, I've walked that mile and I do understand grief, and I think it probably makes me a little bit more empathetic towards the victims of car accidents.

A big part of our program is seeing people at home with their family. So as well as following Chris at work, we shot a sequence of him teaching his then sixteen-year-old daughter Lauren to drive, and filmed a family dinner.

Most importantly, we had the opportunity to get to know Chris's wife, Trish, and she agreed to talk to us on camera. The life of a police officer is difficult at the best of times, and Trish Ferguson had been through more than her fair share of worrying about her husband's career.

'I have regularly prepared myself for Chris's death ever since I married him. I rehearse in my mind what I'd do if it was him and I'd then cope with the aftermath of that.'

Nothing could have prepared Trish Ferguson for the stress her family would suffer when her husband was charged with murder, or how it would continue to affect her for many years to come. I found out later that Trish had suffered migraine headaches, brought on by stress, ever since those traumatic events. But she was so determined to tell her story to us that she refused to take any medication for her headache before the interview. Trish felt she had never had the opportunity to discuss these events publicly and there had been no acknowledgement about what her family had been through. We were about to give her a voice. However, she was adamant that it was Chris's story and she would only talk about it if he would.

We arranged to shoot Chris Ferguson's interview at his home on a Saturday morning. Sitting at his kitchen table, five minutes before the interview was due to start, I asked Chris if he would reconsider talking about the charges as well as his job with the accident squad, as it was obviously something that had had a huge impact on their lives.

He looked at Trish and asked what she thought. Trish's response was yes, he should do it.

Chris and Trish Ferguson talked independently about when they received the news of the murder charges while on holiday with their children in Central Australia. Chris was flown back to Melbourne to face the charges. Trish had to get the car, caravan and kids home on her own.

'I was scared of Chris going to gaol indefinitely,' she said. 'I mean, murder's the big one, twenty years, and police don't fare too well in gaol. I was scared for the children, what sort of future they'd have with their father in gaol.'

Chris Ferguson faced murder charges in Melbourne's Supreme Court with his seven accused co-officers. They were all immediately suspended from the force.

When I was suspended it was a feeling of humiliation, I guess. I was met by two policemen who I knew and they handed me suspension notices on the spot and asked for my badge and identification. And I think that probably hurt the most, you know, because it's every policeman's pride and joy … and to have that taken off you … It's part of your identity and that was a very humiliating experience for me.

Trish had to watch her husband not only face the prospect of a lengthy gaol term, but suffer a huge personal loss with both his parents dying in the two years he was suspended. Chris's father suffered a stroke within three days of the charges being laid. His mother had a heart attack while waiting for her husband in hospital and died eighteen months later. Trish told us she'll always believe their deaths were hastened by the charges.

Despite all this tragedy, Chris Ferguson said that he had never considered not going back to the job he loved, and every day he'd wished he was working as a policeman again. While he was suspended, he made use of his time and went to university. The subjects he studied then helped him get the job in charge of the Accident Investigation Section when he eventually returned to the police force.

The nightmare finally came to an end when the Director of Public Prosecutions, Geoffrey Flatman, decided there was 'no reasonable prospect of conviction' and the charges were dropped. Chris Ferguson said that he felt like a 'fish out of water' when he was reinstated as a policeman and it took a long time for his confidence and self-esteem to come back.

'I don't know if you ever get over the anger of why it happened, but I've dealt with it. And to this day no one's ever told us the reasons as to why we were charged.'

'In the Line of Duty' went to air in July 1998. Chris told me later that finally being able to talk about their ordeal had been an incredibly cathartic experience, particularly for Trish, as she felt no one had ever recognised what their family had gone through, or apologised for it. Now the Fergusons felt they were able to resolve a great deal of the post-traumatic stress and tension in their lives, which had almost ended their marriage.

Chris Ferguson has since been promoted to Chief Inspector of Transit Police and is now a Superintendent in charge of a large area of Victoria. By all accounts he is still what he always wanted to be — a good policeman.

Professor Robert Tindle with his daughter, Danielle, who survived Hodgkin's lymphoma.

In Professor Tindle's Fridge

Professor Robert Tindle

Danielle Tindle was diagnosed with Hodgkin's
lymphoma at the age of twenty-two. Her father,
Professor Robert Tindle, tells of his remarkable
response to Danielle's life-threatening illness.
One which led Danielle to see him in a wholly
different light …

Before Danielle became ill we had a fairly typical 'concerned father/flippant daughter' relationship. A daughter who wanted to experience everything in the world and a father who would bite his tongue at the size of a phone bill and occasionally bawl her out for some misdemeanour. Apparently she used to call me a brain-dead retard from an alien planet … At one point, she left home and didn't tell us where she was going or who she was living with; she just disappeared.

Danielle had been feeling tired and run-down for a while, but put it down to her 'work hard, play hard' approach. She was a student at that point. Then one day she felt a lump on her neck. It turned out there were three lumps in total, one on her neck, a larger lump in the middle of her chest, and another smaller one in her upper abdomen. Her oncologist, Dr Devinder Gill, told us it was Hodgkin's lymphoma — a life-threatening illness.

They treated the disease with chemotherapy and radiotherapy and Danielle achieved remission. However, after a short while the tumour came back much worse than before. When relapses such as this occur, the standard form of treatment is a rather more severe form of chemotherapy but the outcome, I'm afraid, was very bad. There was virtually no response of the tumour to this chemotherapy. Dr Gill came to the conclusion that high-dose chemotherapy followed by stem-cell rescue would be Danielle's best option.

One day shortly after this decision had been made, Anthony Steele, the nurse involved in taking stem cells from Danielle, was explaining to Danielle exactly what was involved and I was at the table reading my research papers and I think he thought I wasn't showing much interest so eventually he looked up and said, 'Have you got any questions for me?' and I had to say, 'Well, Anthony, actually I was on the team which helped first discover the stem cells in the blood. I don't think I have any questions, but thank you very much.'

That's when Danielle found out that I had discovered CD34s — blood stem cells — back in 1984. At that point it seems I became a lot more interesting to Danielle. She says it was a very strange experience for her, realising that the technology that she was experiencing at the time was the result of her own father's discovery.

Throughout my career I've been involved in how you can make the immune response cope with the foreignness of tumours. When I was working in the UK in the late 70s, one of the things that my group turned up was a particular reagent which, it turns out, could identify stem cells in bone marrow. Just as we made this discovery, the research fund got cut. I had the reagent in this little fridge at home and I'd use my unemployment benefit to send it off to all the main centres in Europe and reports kept coming back saying it identified stem cells. What emerged was, hey, look, we can identify a cell that you can give to people whose blood systems and immune systems have been wiped out, which will rescue them.

The stem-cell rescue meant that Danielle had to go through a seven-day concoction of very aggressive chemicals that basically knocked out her entire lymphatic system.

We were pretty close to a toxicity which could kill the tumour but could also kill Danielle. Bilirubin is normally supposed to be under 20 in people with normally functioning livers, but hers was 570. The toxicity was too much for Danielle's system and her liver failed.

Danielle was at the stage where she couldn't struggle any more. I remember that as the worst night: her bilirubin hit 570 and it was getting worse. Most people don't survive if it's at the 500 mark. She was as close to death as she could get. I have no religious persuasion whatsoever, but I will freely admit that the emotional side of me succumbs to praying. The corridors of oncology wards at midnight can be devastating places, devastating and lonely places, and there were several occasions when my tears flowed. But I'd get over that and the next day I'd be back into 'Right, what have we got to do today?' mode, the objective mode.

Then, slowly, her bilirubin came back down until, several months later, it was normal. Dr Gill said it was one of the most remarkable recoveries he had seen in twenty-five years and that it was probably the stem-cell transplant that cured the disease.

Elizabeth, my wife, thinks it was amazing that these things that we had had in our fridge — twenty years later — contributed greatly to saving our own daughter's life.

Because of the possibility of relapse, we discussed the possibility of what's called immunotherapy. This isn't a standard therapy; it's experimental. We sent Danielle's blood to Houston (where there was a clinical trial running at Baylor College of Medicine) where they extracted the T-cells and educated them to kill her tumour. We also took skin cells from Danielle and worked on them for a number of months before sending those to Houston, too. They were engineered to look like tumour cells to see if the T-cells would kill them. To our delight, we got an email back telling us they did, which meant if Houston put those T-cells back into Danielle, then there would be a very good chance that those cells would go around her body, home in on any residual tumour she had left then clear it out of her body. Danielle and I flew over to Houston immediately. The cells were re-implanted into her on two occasions. Dr Bollard (of Baylor College) says that they don't know if the therapy cured Danielle but that they've had promising results from the ten patients they've treated so far.

The outcome of this approach is going to be beneficial, not just for those with Hodgkin's lymphoma, but to all people who have tumours where there is a foreign antigen into which a killer T-cell population can be directed.

Making an *Australian Story* about Danielle's illness was a pretty intense experience for our family and for the people at the hospital: the doctors and nurses, because we had to relive the whole wretched thing. There were a lot of buried emotions that came to the surface that were more intense in some ways than the emotions which occurred at the time of Danielle's whole disease process, treatment and recovery, which rather surprised me.

It also brought up some interesting interactions in the family. I can imagine that in other, perhaps less closely knit and switched on families, you could have had a lot of family discord occurring; you could see how in some families it could become an issue.

There's a lot of good things that have come out of the program.

First of all, a couple of people have subsequently phoned up and made donations to research. Another positive thing that's come out of the program is one of the things that the Princess Alexandra Hospital (where Danielle was treated) did. The Nurse Manager, Gillian Myles advised oncology nurses within Queensland, that they should really watch the show. A lot of them did and one of the outcomes is that the hospital has received many requests, from oncology nurses to do their training there.

The day the program went to air I was extremely apprehensive for two reasons. The first reason was a professional reason: it's extremely important that there was no misrepresentation in the program and that any comments that I'd made on the scientific or medical aspects of the program were not misrepresented, that everything was in context and that neither myself nor Dr Gill were quoted out of context.

And the second reason was that the whole thing was fairly intense emotionally, and I was worried as to how the whole thing was going to pan out. I was keen to see that every member of the family and all of those people who participated in the story be allowed to have their say. I didn't want the program to concentrate too much on the 'my father, my daughter', kind of thing and not give due recognition to other people who played vital roles. But I think the producer, Caitlin Shea, got it just about exactly right and everyone got their fair dues.

On the night it screened we simply sat down as a family and watched it with rapt attention. Danielle got a bit emotional when she was watching it, and afterwards we analysed it a bit. We were very pleasantly surprised at the outcome. We've had enormous amount of feedback from friends and relatives, and you wouldn't believe the number of people who've stopped Danielle or me in the street and said, 'Oh, we saw your story and we thought it was great'.

There was one nice little thing that happened two days after the program was shown. I had to head over to Vancouver to a medical conference and was sitting in the Qantas lounge, waiting from my flight, and some Qantas staff came up to us and said,

'Oh, we saw your story the other night and it was absolutely wonderful, we're so proud of you', and they upgraded me to business class, which was pretty nice.

So if you want to get upgraded to business class, that's what you have to do. Get yourself on *Australian Story* and sit in the Qantas lounge …

I know Danielle may well relapse. Of course, down to the depths of my shoes I hope it doesn't occur and I suspect it won't. But if it does occur, I know we've got the strength to cope with it. We don't worry about it at the moment. During the period of Danielle's illness a phenomenal bond was established between us. There's a sense of having experienced something together. Nothing that happens to us subsequently will be able to dissolve that.

Every loving father gives of his all for his kids. You'll give everything you've got and that's what I've done. I've given everything I've got.

Professor Robert Tindle and his daughter Danielle at the virus research centre at the Royal Children's Hospital. Professor Tindle led the stem cell research which saved Danielle's life.

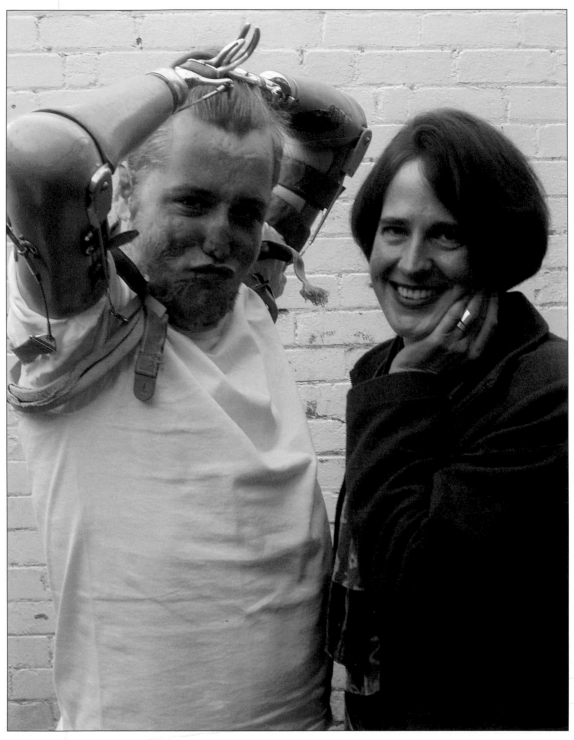

Tom Nash and producer Rebecca Latham in Tom's backyard, Sydney, June 2005.

While You Were Sleeping

Rebecca Latham

Tom Nash was a happy, healthy university student in 2001, when he started to feel unwell with classic common cold symptoms. A couple of days later, he was in hospital fighting for his life. Doctors diagnosed a severe case of meningococcal disease and told his parents he was unlikely to survive. But against all odds, Tom pulled through — minus four limbs and with skin grafts covering half his body.

In 2003, *Australian Story* teamed up with Tom as he put the pieces of his life back together.

I felt very nervous about meeting Tom Nash. We were driving through the Blue Mountains west of Sydney, heading towards the house where he lived with his mother. Sitting beside me in the car was reporter Mark Horstman, who had just aired a story about Tom on ABC Radio National's *Health Report* program. The piece had struck *Australian Story*'s Executive Producer, Deb Fleming, who thought it might make good television.

Mark had generously arranged a meeting with Tom and agreed to introduce me.

Tom Nash survived an illness that should have killed him. Meningococcal septicaemia is a disease that sounds like something out of the Dark Ages. A virulent bug, with symptoms dangerously similar to the common cold, it can kill a perfectly healthy person in a few hours. Just days after his nineteenth birthday, Tom was on life support in Sydney's Royal Prince Alfred Hospital. His limbs were turning gangrenous and he'd had two heart attacks. Doctors told his parents to prepare for the worst. Instead, Tom defied medical expectations and pulled through. But the price he paid was enormous. To stay alive, he chose to become a quadruple amputee. I was on my way to meet a man who had no arms or legs.

This was something that worried me. It's well known in journalism that programs about illness and death — other people's misfortunes — attract a big audience. *Australian Story* had done lots of pieces around this time on people who'd lost limbs, grown up in wheelchairs, overcome a debilitating illness. They were all great programs about very special individuals — but did we need another? I was worried we'd be making a sensationalist show about somebody too vulnerable to resist.

Mark Horstman didn't seem to think so. As we drove, he sketched an intriguing portrait of Tom Nash as a man who didn't see himself as a victim, who didn't want pity and who retained a wicked sense of humour. He warned me that Tom's tactic on meeting people was to confront them straightaway with his disability and then make a tasteless joke — preferably at his own expense. 'He likes to shake hands,' Mark said. 'So you'll have to shake hooks.'

Tom's voicemail message had been interesting too. It ran something like: 'Yeah, this is Tom. Leave a message and I might call you back.' Then he'd added, 'If I feel like it,' and rang off with a barely audible cackle.

Tom was waiting for us on the porch. As we walked up the steps, he levered himself from his seat to stand and greet us. There was no wheelchair in sight. True to Mark's prediction, he waved a laconic hook in my direction. As I drew nearer, I noticed 'love' inscribed across one hook and 'hate' on the other. It made me think of a high school tattoo; a reminder that, despite what he'd been through, Tom was only twenty years old.

I found his appearance startling. Purple scars criss-crossed his face, a legacy of the septicaemia that accompanied the meningitis. He looked like a burns victim. (Tom told me later that people would ask in the street if he'd got the scars in the Bali bombings.) Strapped beneath his knees were prosthetics that ended in a flexible metal bar, duplicating the rolling action of a foot. These 'feet' were enclosed inside a pair of black lace-up shoes. There were hooks where his hands had been, attached to artificial forearms. Tom could activate the pincer action of the hooks — similar to the grasping action of a thumb and forefinger — by flicking his elbow.

'Light me a cigarette, will you?' he asked Mark as we sat down.

Mark fitted the cigarette into his hook and Tom raised it to his mouth. He had the whole sequence down pat, apart from the difficulty of flicking the lighter. It was clear the veranda was where he spent a lot of his time.

'It's the only place where Mum lets me smoke,' he explained, as he saw me looking at the overflowing ashtray and the coffee cups fitted with straws.

Later, when we knew each other better, I asked about the chain-smoking. Tom's justification was simple. 'If meningococcal disease can't kill me, I'll have to find something that can!'

My main concern that day was to find out whether Tom would be up to the challenge of making a program with *Australian Story*. It takes a long time to gather material, and the process is emotionally and physically demanding. But as we talked, my doubts began to settle. Tom was obviously not the kind of person to stay at home in a wheelchair, hidden from prying eyes. He wasn't embarrassed by his physical disabilities, he said, and he didn't see why anyone else should be either. I summoned some courage at this point and asked how people reacted to him. His answer was frank and matter-of-fact.

> Most people look at you and then look away, which is really interesting. You wonder why people just don't come up and ask you what happened, because I'm obviously OK with it because I'm walking around … It's not a big deal. I think the political correctness lobby has a lot to do with that. You know, don't offend people, say the right thing, look but don't stare.

One agenda for doing the program, he said, was to educate people about the disease and how to prevent it. He'd already built a public profile in this area, promoting a vaccine for one of the meningococcal strains. And because it's a disease that singles out children and young adults, he'd done school speeches about his experience. Simply, he was passionate about not wanting anybody else to go through the same experience he did.

He wasn't sure, though, he said, that he was the right material for *Australian Story*. 'Why?' I asked.

The humility of his answer stunned me. 'I thought you did heroic stories. I'm just, like, a guy who's gone through something. When you think about it, I haven't really done much.'

This statement, I realised later, was vintage Tom: self-deprecating to a fault. Despite surviving multiple amputations and a gruelling rehabilitation, he was seriously telling me he was nothing special!

At the time that we met, Tom's life consisted of a dizzying array of visits to prosthetic specialists, physiotherapists, psychiatrists and doctors. In the downtime, he worked on perfecting the everyday tasks most of us take for granted. Simple things, like using a computer or a phone, represented hours of frustrating hit and miss as Tom retrained himself to use hooks instead of hands.

Handles, cups, CDs — anything that failed to cooperate was subjected to an unending stream of insults.

One day I encountered Tom standing at a door, addressing the doorknob: 'OK, you c——. So you're not going to do it? We'll see about that, you c——-s———-!'

Tom's tirade at the doorknob would have been a perfect moment to film. It summed up completely the frustrations with his new body in a way that words could never do. Alas, the camera was nowhere in sight. The moment disappeared and during the actual interview Tom insisted on describing his frustrations in a tamer fashion.

It's a constant adaptation when you find new things that you used to be able to do that you can't do any more. It gets really frustrating. I was making a cup of coffee and I thought, all right, I can turn the kettle on like I used to, I can get a cup out. I got halfway through and I thought, how am I going to pour the jug? Oh fuck. And then I had to call someone in, which was useless because I could have got them to do all the rest of it anyway!

Although he didn't say so, I got the impression that Tom saw a film about his life to date as a kind of vindication — recognition of all he'd been through. And, despite the busy physical rehabilitation timetable, he was still putting in long hours on the veranda, smoking cigarettes and watching the world go by. He was bored and an attentive film crew offered a welcome distraction.

His ultimate goal, he told me, was to reclaim his old life. A talented musician and guitarist, his plan was to learn to play another instrument with his hooks, go back to university and share a house with friends. In the meantime, he was living quietly in the Blue Mountains with his mother, Marilyn, who was helping him every step of the way.

Marilyn had put the rest of her life on hold to support Tom through his illness. 'It's been very hard,' she admitted over coffee and cakes that day. 'As soon as Tom got the meningococcal, my life just basically stopped. Earnings have been nil, basically nil, and I've just gone through my life savings.'

Relentlessly optimistic, Marilyn had clearly played a crucial role in Tom's recovery. She was determined to help him become independent.

> I'm not a depressed type of person. I don't sit there and carry on and cry about it, that wouldn't do any good. We've got to be positive around him. It's no good if you sit around crying and carrying on and woe is us and look at you — he would go downhill. That's not going to get anybody anywhere.

I left the house that day inspired by Tom's story. His courage and will to live, combined with a charismatic personality and forceful intelligence, formed a unique mixture. The thing I found most compelling was that, despite having lost all his limbs, he'd somehow learned to walk again. Marilyn had shown me a tape that day which became vital footage in the program. Filmed a few months earlier, it captured Tom's first steps. The agonised look on his face as he shuffled forwards in a frame, bearing his full body weight on stumps covered with scar tissue, was humbling to watch. But in the midst of all that pain and suffering, flanked by encouraging medical staff and family, he'd still found time to lighten the moment.

'First of all I'd like to thank God,' he droned, deadpan, to the camera, 'for getting me here today. And I'd like to thank my parents …'

Mark Horstman's *Health Report* program had focused on the medical side of Tom's story. But buried deep beneath this account was a more personal, emotive story about a teenage boy and his struggle with a terrifying disease. I wanted to tell that story, to find out what made Tom tick. At the same time, I didn't want to gloss over the nitty-gritty of his experience. Tom obviously had extraordinary courage, but this wasn't a story with a neat and happy ending — an 'up' ending in *Australian Story* parlance. How did he find the strength to get through this experience; the mental discipline to cope with its brutal legacy, day in and day out?

Marilyn summed it up best.

He faces it every day, you know, it's a very hard thing. He is the one who lies there in the night-time with his prosthetics off. If you ever placed yourself in that position, how would you feel to lay in a bed without the bottom half of your arms and the bottom half of your legs? There's nothing wrong with your brain, you know, there's nothing wrong with any other part of you, but the excess part of your limbs have been cut off.

It was a haunting image — Tom immobilised in bed night after night, unable to move until someone came in to get him up — and it returned to me over and over while we were filming. I never did summon the courage to speak to him about it though. Asking what Tom's private thoughts were as he lay in bed each night felt too personal — like crossing a line. As a producer, finding the balance between the needs of the story and respecting a subject's privacy is often the toughest part of the job. In Tom's case, I found myself constantly pulling back from questions that might sound insensitive.

As we drove back to Sydney that afternoon, Mark and I talked excitedly about how we could film the program. We knew the story wouldn't be easy to tell. Many of Tom's most crucial experiences had been and gone without a film crew in attendance: the emergency period in the hospital, his long months in rehab. It certainly wasn't the best time to get the camera out of the box.

We were faced with the evils of filming what we call the 'recreation': finding a way to illustrate large chunks of Tom's 'back story' — the things that happened before we met him. To get these sequences, we'd have to return to the hospitals where Tom had spent a year of his life and recreate some of the key events. In a further complication, there wasn't much archival material available: some photos of Tom and two short home videos — one showing him playing guitar at a school concert, and the other at a family dinner. Also preying on my mind was the sense of a major family issue, bubbling under the surface. I didn't understand what it was about and assumed that at some point things would get clearer. Ultimately, not many secrets survive the filming process.

The first step was to piece together the narrative. Understanding the chronology is crucial when you make an *Australian Story* program. In the absence of a voice-over, the interviews provide the only explanation of what's going on. Woe betide the producer who enters an interview unprepared! If you forget to ask a question, you can end up with huge holes in the story.

Tom told me he'd contracted the meningococcal disease during celebrations for his nineteenth birthday. The disease spreads via saliva and can be contracted any number of ways: sharing cigarettes, drinking from the same bottle or kissing are just a few of the possibilities. He was living alone, working part-time and studying at university. Nobody was with him when the first signs appeared.

> I was feeling chronically tired. If you've ever been up three days in a row and just really need to get to sleep and you're as full as a boot, like that's how I felt. I woke up in the night feeling really cold, especially my hands and feet, like I had frostbite. In the morning, I couldn't fit my shoes on my feet because they were so swollen, and I thought, this is ridiculous, I'm going to go and see a doctor.

Tom phoned his stepsister, Frances Cucinotta, who lived nearby. Frances told us:

> He said, 'Can you call me tomorrow to see if I'm still alive?' Tom being Tom, I thought, ha ha, it's a joke. When he eventually let me in he was standing in the shadows and as he stepped back into the light he had a purple light all over his body. I took him to the nearest hospital and they rushed him to intensive care. He waved goodbye and that was the last time he waved goodbye to me or to anyone.

The prognosis was grim. Despite being sick for just a few hours, Tom was now dangerously ill. The early symptoms of meningococcal disease are similar to those of a common cold, making it difficult for doctors to diagnose. In addition, Tom had contracted two different diseases: meningitis, an inflammation of the brain's lining; and septicaemia, which is blood poisoning. The alarming purple rash Frances saw when Tom opened the door was a sign that the blood poisoning had taken hold.

I put in a bid to speak to one of Tom's doctors at Royal Prince Alfred Hospital in Sydney, and to do some filming in the intensive care unit. It's very difficult to film in ICUs: patients are extremely sick and there are major issues to do with confidentiality and privacy. However, Tom had made such an impact on the people who treated him that they didn't mind helping us. This reaction to Tom was something I came across again and again during the filming process.

After we'd recreated some scenes in the ICU, I sat down to interview Tom's treating doctor, Robert Herkes. He said it was one of the worst cases he'd ever come across. 'We told him he was extremely sick. Had he asked me, I would have said that his chance of survival was only ten or twenty per cent. The most likely thing was that he was going to die.'

Tom's chances of survival were so minimal that before he fell unconscious Herkes asked if he'd consider trying an unproven drug on clinical trial at the hospital. Tom agreed and the drug — Activated Protein C — was incorporated into his treatment. The next few days, said Herkes, were 'a stormy course', as Tom battled for his life.

Tom suffered multiple organ failure and two heart attacks. His parents were told to prepare for the worst. His father, Peter Nash, vividly described the frightening days at his son's bedside.

'Thomas had bloated up to double his normal size. There was more equipment attached to him than I've seen in any TV program. He was on full life support. A lot of things are going through your mind in terms of, my God, how long have we got, can you say goodbye to him. It was a horror period of going through what would life be like without Thomas and, I suppose, what would life be if he was to survive and what were the implications of this disease.'

Against all odds, the intensive care staff triumphed. Two weeks later, Tom woke from his coma. It's generally acknowledged that the Activated Protein C played a crucial — although unknown — role in his survival. But Peter Nash was right to worry about his son's future quality of life. His parents had lived with the impact of his illness for the previous two weeks, but for Tom himself, the understanding of his changed physical state was just beginning.

When I woke up I realised I couldn't move my arms or legs. I was on so many drugs you don't really question what's happened to you … My feet were really dark black and I thought, jeez, that's gonna take a while to come off, and then my arms the same, and then after a while I realised that the blackness actually came to the top of my thigh and I started to get a bit worried about it but still didn't know what was going to happen.

Dr Robert Herkes described Tom's arms and legs as being in a 'parlous state'. Although he was off life support, his muscles were continuing to die. For Herkes and the other medical staff, the prospect of future amputations led to some agonised soul-searching. Had their aggressive intervention to save Tom been for the best? Herkes said:

I guess one of the things as a doctor that always concerns me when I see a patient like Tom survive, but survive with a great disability, is how he's going to cope for the next twenty or thirty years, to lose all your limbs presents huge difficulties … He is a lad who had his life in front of him, was off to university. Who in the end has lost his limbs … he's going to end up being dependent on others for the rest of his life. It makes us wonder whether we're doing the appropriate thing keeping him alive but burdening him with a lot of illness and future dependency.

Tom was transferred from Royal Prince Alfred to the burns unit at Concord Hospital, in Sydney's west, to receive multiple skin grafts on the areas where his skin had been eaten away by septicaemia. There, he faced the worst decision of his life.

The doctor came into my room and said, 'Oh, your legs are going to have to come off.' I said, 'Is there a way of saving them?' And he said, 'Yeah, but you'll die.' You think, OK, take them off. I think the human willpower to live is much stronger. We all pretty much underestimate it.

Tom talked about this devastating decision during our first interview. I'd decided to record two interviews with him: one at the beginning of the shoot and one at the end. The first would give me the narrative structure and chronology; the second would be an opportunity to delve deeper into Tom's psyche. I didn't want to pry, but at the same time I — and the audience — needed some clues about how he'd found the strength of mind to survive.

So far, the filming was going well. Although Tom was open and cooperative, it was clear he was also a born exhibitionist, hamming it up as soon as the camera was turned on. Finding the real Tom — the person behind the ironical exterior that had sustained him through his nightmare experiences — looked like it might be difficult.

I'd already seen that humour was a vital ingredient in his get-well mix. Prior to the first interview, we'd filmed a sequence in a Katoomba café with Tom and Keith (his friend and carer) eating lunch. Tom digressed into a hysterically funny aside about a speech he was planning to give on meningococcal disease to a school. Why not include a Tom Nash show bag, he suggested, with plastic hooks, stick-on scars and chocolate koalas with the arms and legs bitten off? And then — to the consternation of passers-by — he'd manoeuvred his fork towards his face and deliberately splattered food across his forehead.

The way Peter Nash saw it, humour was Tom's secret weapon.

Thomas has got a very dry and satirical sense of humour. He always has had. Many times he'll come up with things that make fun of him in a way, but he's trying to make you feel at ease — don't worry about the fact I'm severely disabled, it's not your fault and please behave as normally as you can around me … Funnily enough, he doesn't see himself as a victim.

When the time came for Tom to make a decision about amputating his arms, humour was in short supply. The guitar was his passion in life and losing his hands was a brutal destruction of hope. Without them, he faced a whole new realm of disability: suddenly, his future prospects shifted from being relatively independent — perhaps in a wheelchair, but mostly able to fend for himself — to being completely dependent on carers.

'It was just a nightmare,' said Peter Nash. 'It just became … the arms, the legs, what's next. I mean, there's not much left in terms of limbs obviously.'

I knew Tom had been through a prolonged depression at that point. And that he'd considered suicide. The tragic irony was, with his arms gone he couldn't do it alone.

For Marilyn, it was an unbearable decision. 'He would say, if I really loved him, I would actually help him to die. And he'd plead with me. I said, I will not do it, as a mother.'

Peter Nash was more resolute.

He got to the point where he really did not wish to go on. In terms of decisions to help him potentially end his life, if that's what he wanted, I was going to support whatever he wanted to do.

As we settled down for the final interview in Marilyn's Blue Mountains home, I knew we had to ask Tom about the period where he wanted to die. I felt that Tom and I were as relaxed with each other as we were ever going to be. It was time to dig a little deeper.

Before she left that morning, Marilyn had told me it wouldn't be easy. 'Try all you like,' she said. 'But he calls all the shots. Even with his psychiatrist.' And then, with a hint of bitterness, 'He controls everything.'

Marilyn was right. Tom's trauma was so immense, there were definite no-go zones. Whenever he found a question too problematic, he'd answer in monosyllables. The interview progressed in stops and starts, a bit like a chess game: approach and retreat, approach and retreat. To make matters worse, we were bedevilled with technical problems. A bulb in one of the lights blew, shorting an electrical circuit. While the crew were out at the car looking for a new bulb, I noticed rivulets of sweat running down Tom's face.

'I think my blood sugar's getting a bit low,' he said. 'Can we go outside and have a cigarette?'

There was no option but to let go of the interview thread. I made him a Vegemite sandwich and helped him down the stairs to the backyard. I'd forgotten that because many of Tom's sweat glands disappeared with the amputations, his body found it impossible to regulate extremes of heat. For previous filming, we'd used the minimum of lights or natural light. But this time we'd forgotten — and Tom was too polite to remind us.

As we stood in the backyard, Tom chain-smoking and me lighting his cigarettes as usual, I apologised guiltily. 'Yeah, don't worry about it,' he said.

We surveyed the overgrown yard in silence. At the end of the driveway was a shed. Inside, I knew, were Tom's guitars. Marilyn had mentioned them earlier. 'All his stuff is in there,' she'd said. 'I can't bring myself to go through it.' As I fed Tom bites of sandwich, I realised, finally, that the key to his recovery was never to go back. There were to be no lonely moments in the garage. No retreats allowed. Just keep moving forward.

I watched him balancing on his artificial legs, facing into the wind. The scars across his face and misshapen ears paled slightly in the cold. As he flicked his elbow to manoeuvre the cigarette to his mouth there was a distinctive clunking sound from the artificial joint and I remembered something he'd told me earlier. Originally, he'd wanted hands that looked less artificial. But despite the confronting appearance of the hooks, he came to realise they were much easier to use.

With what was by now a familiar pun, he'd said, 'I used to be really hooked on aesthetic value. I wanted hands that looked realistic. Now I just don't give a shit. If this is going to make me more functional, then I'm going to wear these, rather than try and force someone into thinking that you haven't lost your limbs.'

I realised this attitude summed Tom up. It didn't matter if the hooks alarmed people. To hell with what they might think. To survive, he'd made peace with his appearance. It was this philosophy that allowed him to walk down the street, immune to the stares and whispers. And it was the same positive attitude that had pulled him out of his depression in the hospital and turned his thoughts away from suicide. He was, quite simply, the most courageous person I had ever met.

Deaf to my thoughts, Tom stubbed out his cigarette. 'Should get on with it,' he said. And then, 'Think this place needs a *Backyard Blitz* job. You reckon Channel Nine might come up? Give Mum a surprise.'

We shot our last segment for the film a few days later. Tom had kept up with his music and was singing in a band with some mates. The guitar was temporarily by the wayside, he told me, although, 'I might learn to play it with my hooks'.

One by one his friends turned up, carting equipment, and we set up the shoot in a soundproof rehearsal room. The plan was to use this sequence as the opening to the film because Tom was writing a lot of the music himself. I intended to intercut it with archival footage of him as a schoolboy, playing guitar at a school concert. It seemed a good example of how far he'd come and — perhaps — how far he was going to go.

In between takes, Tom harangued his mates about the quality of their playing and they hassled him good-naturedly about needing voice lessons. Afterwards, we went to a pub to celebrate finishing the shoot.

There were a few surprises after the story went to air. The family issue I'd been wondering about earlier came to the fore, when Marilyn expressed her view about the program. In an unexpected response, she told me she was unhappy with the finished product, she felt her role as Tom's primary carer and nurturer had been under-recognised.

Because Tom's parents were separated, I'd been dealing primarily with Marilyn. However, at Tom's request, I'd recorded an interview with his father, Peter, who had kept vigil by his son's bedside along with the rest of his extended family. Peter had provided many valuable insights into Tom's illness and recovery, but Marilyn's view was that he'd featured too prominently in the story — to her detriment.

I realised we were treading on shaky ground, some of it relating, perhaps, to a difficult separation between Tom's parents sixteen years ago. Marilyn's reaction was subjective but understandable, and it reminded me how easy it is for our subjects to experience a loss of control during the filming process. The relationship between producer and subject can be very intense. After all, people are trusting us with their deepest secrets and their most emotional moments. Sometimes, the assumption is made (but rarely explicitly stated) that we're telling the story exclusively from one person's point of view. Although it's true that the stories are highly personal, it is commonplace to speak to family and friends to flesh out the details — which, of course, was what happened in Tom's case.

Tom's own attitude to the program was overwhelmingly positive. Sanguine about his mother's reaction, he stressed that he was happy the program featured other members of his extended family. When I caught up with him in early 2005, he reminisced about the impact of the story. The newfound fame, he said, was the hardest thing to deal with.

> It had a weird effect. I'd go out in public and people would say, you're that guy from *Australian Story*. It happened all the time. You can't get angry with them. They've got good intentions. But it gives you the shits after a while!

He's an older, grungier-looking Tom these days. A bit harder and a bit more cynical. His hair is long and a beard covers the scars on his face. As we sat in his local pub, I marvelled at his progress. He perched comfortably on a bar stool, easily manipulating a coffee cup towards his mouth — something that would have been impossible two years ago when we were filming.

We talked about what he was up to. He's fulfilled his dream of living independently and shares a house with a friend. Carers visit him in the morning and help him to bed each night. But for the remainder of the day, he fends for himself. Music is a huge part of his life: his band is getting regular Sydney gigs and his plan is to set up a music production company. In the meantime, he's studying music business management. He's had lots of follow-up media attention from the *Australian Story* program, including a documentary that's now in post-production.

'I know I'm lucky to have survived,' he told me, 'but where do you draw the line on luck? One could say it's good luck that you survived, but people could also say it's bad luck because you've lost all your limbs. I don't believe in luck. It's just what happens. This is what happened to me and the main thing is you've got to make the best of it.'

Daniel's parents Bruce and Denise Morcombe appeal for help.

A Life-changing Experience

Claire Forster

Australian Story touches people's lives in all kinds

of ways — and it's not only the subjects who are

affected. Viewers often feel personally touched by

the people they 'meet' on screen, and frequently ask

questions about their ongoing welfare. *Australian Story*

is quite simply 'must watch' television for many people

I meet. And it has a huge impact on those of us who

work on it as well. For me, it's changed the whole

direction of my life.

In May 1996, when I was working on the 7.30 *Report* in Sydney, I was invited to watch the first broadcast of a show which Head of News and Current Affairs, Paul Williams, predicted would become one of the flagship programs of the ABC. The opening credits rolled and within minutes I was hooked. My dream of becoming an overseas correspondent, reporting on wars, famines and international crises, disappeared that night as I watched the very first *Australian Story*.

I rang executive producer Deb Fleming many times over the years, hoping for an opportunity to work on her team, and finally it happened. It was a six-week secondment and the story I was to produce was on eighteen-year-old classical pianist Simon Tedeschi.

Just shy of his sixth birthday, Simon Tedeschi heard a boy play the piano and within minutes decided he wanted to be a concert pianist. He played at the Sydney Opera House when he was only nine, and by the age of ten was no longer attending most classes — his teachers allowed him to rehearse instead. By the time of our program, Simon had played all around the world, and his hands had starred in the movie *Shine* as those of a young David Helfgott.

I remember walking into Simon's home, which he shared with his mother, young brother and sister — and his piano. The instrument was a central character in the family's life and took up most of the lounge room. Simon's siblings were unable to use the room when he was practising, which meant the lounge was forbidden territory for several hours each day.

Simon spoke about his connection with the piano in his interview. 'The piano has become not so much an instrument but an integral part of me so together we become a whole. It's my self-esteem, it's my psyche, it's my personality and when I play the piano I play beautiful piano, I don't just play the piano.'

Simon's mother, Vivienne, explained the emotional seesaw of having a genius in the family.

'The first time he played with a proper symphony orchestra, and he came out and I realised that he would have to stand to play this concerto because he wouldn't get to the top and the bottom of the keyboard unless he was half-standing. And my heart sank and I wished he wasn't doing it at that moment. It didn't seem fair to put a little child through this. It was okay once he was doing it, but there's just that moment that I used to think, why are we all doing this and why can't we just go home and be normal?'

Our *Australian Story* program delved into the demands Simon's talent had made on his family and the inevitable strains that had developed.

Simon's father, NSW Crown Prosecutor Mark Tedeschi — a man well known for his prosecutions of high-profile criminal cases, including the Hilton bombing and the Milat backpacker murders — had left the family many years before. Simon was clearly affected by the distant relationship he had with his father.

Pianist Simon Tedeschi, 2000.

> I don't have a relationship with my father ... this is my choice. It was quite a one-sided thing. It was one person that chose to leave and it was the rest of the family that was left clinging for support like hanging from a cliff.

Simon was an interesting subject, obviously highly talented and intelligent, but also a very complex teenager. He nominated his thirty-eight-year-old manager, Patrick Togher, as his closest friend — and while he pined for his lost childhood, he seemed only slightly concerned that he was also missing his teenage years.

He confessed that several times he had 'broken out' from the intense life of a concert pianist. When he was thirteen he called the same phone number 1009 times — resulting in a trip to Chatswood police station.

It was embarrassing for my father … with his public position he found it very threatening. The police informed me that if I even breathed out of time again I'd find myself sort of sharing a cell … or something … I've played for Commissioner Ryan recently. He didn't seem to know of my past offences.

I thought Simon was funny — very different from your average teenager, but also very likeable. I hoped our story conveyed that.

The morning after 'A Genius in the Family' aired, I took part in the producers' phone hook-up — a weekly occurrence during which everyone discusses the previous night's story. It's a call that is often feared — colleagues don't hold back and can often be quite critical. I came off the line feeling shattered: nearly every single producer had said they hadn't 'warmed' to Simon; they either didn't like him or didn't understand him. I felt as if I had failed Simon.

Worse was to come. While Simon's manager liked the story, Simon himself was angry — he felt the story focused too much on his father — and he refused to talk to me. I was mortified. Later I heard that Simon had publicly criticised the program and me.

It was a baptism of fire for me as a producer.

Given that my first program had been less than universally loved, I was unsure whether I would be working on *Australian Story* again. However, just as I was about to jet off on overseas holiday, I got a call from Brigid Donovan, an friend who was producing on *Australian Story*. She asked whether I would be able to do some filming for her with a group of school students while I was in France. I agreed immediately.

'Carve their Names with Pride' told the story of a group of students from North Mackay High School who were visiting the battlefields and cemeteries of Gallipoli and France. They were on a mission to find ninety-eight headstones that marked the death in World War I of men and women who were ancestors of present-day Mackay residents. When the students returned to Mackay, they presented photographs of the gravestones to the siblings, children and grandchildren of those servicemen and women. It was a precious gift as many of the locals had never seen their loved one's last resting place.

Seeing those teenagers standing next to the graves, reading the headstones, being moved to tears and grieving for soldiers they had never met, made me realise once again what a privilege it is to work on a program where people accept your presence during intensely emotional and personal journeys.

Being prepared to work during my holidays was the clincher that got me a full-time position on *Australian Story*. There was just one catch: the position, like the program itself, was based in Brisbane.

My partner, Rodney, is an artist and during that time was endeavouring to get a Sydney gallery to represent him — a mission which would be more difficult from Brisbane. Nevertheless, we made the decision to relocate — or at least, I did. Rodney followed me some months later when he had finished the portrait of classical pianist David Helfgott he was painting to enter in the Archibald Prize.

Australian airman, Chris Jarett.

I was looking for a story when a call came into the office about an eighty-year-old man who might prove an interesting subject. I remember racing into Deb Fleming's office to tell her about this fantastic story — it had everything!

At the age of twenty-four, Australian airman Chris Jarrett was fighting in World War II as part of a Lancaster bomber crew. During a flight over France, the engine failed and the plane crashed. Chris managed to parachute to safety but all six of his mates were killed. He was discovered by some French villagers, who cared for him until he was flown back to his airbase in England twenty-four hours later.

While recuperating in the UK, Chris fell in love with a young Welsh woman. They spoke briefly of marriage, but circumstances conspired against them and Chris returned to Australia alone.

Ten years later, he married Helen and they had a family.

Fast forward fifty years and Chris was forced to part from Helen who was suffering from a condition similar to Alzheimer's disease. Looking after her had become too much for Chris and he'd been persuaded by doctors to move her to a nursing home.

Knowing that the years of caring for Helen had taken their toll on Chris, his daughter Penny asked, 'If you could have one wish, what would it be?' Chris ventured that he would love to return to the village in France where his mates had died and see England again. Penny organised for his wish to come true. And then the fairytale occurred …

Chris recounted it to me. 'Just one week before we were due to fly out, a letter appeared in the *Wings* magazine, which is the magazine of the RAAF Association. And it was a letter to the Editor asking about the whereabouts of John Christie Jarrett. Is he still alive? Anybody knowing his whereabouts could they please get in touch with Joan Burkill. And I rang up the international telephone exchange and got the *telephone* number and rang up and said, "Is that you, Joan?" And she said, "Yes." I said, "This is Chris. I'll be in London in a week's time. "'

Chris caught up with Joan for lunch in Wales, and the two had been corresponding and talking on the phone ever since.

When I spoke to Chris he was organising to return once more to the French town of Thin Le Moutier with a plaque as a final tribute to his six mates who died in the Lancaster crash. *Australian Story*'s budget is small, but I put up a strong argument about flying over to film Chris in France and England — and, thankfully, the bean counters agreed.

The French locals knew of Chris's trip and had arranged a celebration in his honour. The town band, dignitaries and local men, women and children all came to pay tribute to him.

A local woman, Daniele Farey, told us:

All of Thin Le Moutier think their town is more important today
because we have received an Australian pilot. Because in 1945 he
was like a hero for a whole people, especially for French women
because he was a very beautiful man and he was so kindly, and he
was so emotional.

Many of the older townspeople remembered the night the
plane crashed. One man was reduced to tears as he recalled
coming across the dead airmen at the crash scene.

'I didn't think that people would hold little old me in such
regard,' Chris said. 'The whole afternoon was something that I'd
never, ever experienced before. I think one of the greatest, if not
the greatest day I've ever had in my life.'

Chris and some of the locals travelled to the spot where the
bomber came down and, with the aid of metal detectors, actually
found pieces of the plane.

'I miss the crew. I miss them badly,' Chris said. 'I dream about
it even now. But I've done it hundred of times now. I've bailed
out, and I still do.'

Executive Producer Deb Fleming says that a true *Australian
Story* should have all the ingredients of a Shakespearean play.
Chris's story had it all: tragedy, love, conflict, and more. He was
also on a journey of discovery, laying to rest ghosts of the past and
re-evaluating his future — and who he wanted to share it with.

I met up with Chris again in England, while he was visiting
Joan Burkill. A lovely sprightly Welsh woman, what Joan lacked in
height she made up for with personality. She had a great sense of
fun and the spark between the two of them was obvious. Despite
misgivings from some family and friends, Chris had organised to
spend a month with Joan.

After some initial hesitation, Joan agreed to be interviewed.

When he came last year, we only spoke a few hours together and
we would never have recognised each other because we were
both so ancient and wrinkled. And we go, 'Ah, you don't look a bit

different.' I tell a good story. We pull each other's legs; we have a lot of laughs, which is good. And the fifty-five years — just as if they've never been. We just look very different.

The interview was progressing without any hiccups when I asked, 'Did you think about Chris over the years?'

Joan stopped, then said in a choked voice, 'I never forgot him.' Her tiny hands, bent with arthritis, flew to her face and she sobbed. I was horrified, and was trying to think what to say to calm her down when she brought down her hands from her face and added in a quiet voice, 'He says he never forgot me.'

These words went straight to the heart of this story of love and loss. They had a profound effect on me and I knew the audience would respond in the same way. I used them as the very last frames of the film.

I watched the finished program at ABC Headquarters in Sydney with Chris Jarrett and his family. I was nervous. I thought the film was good but what if Chris — like Simon Tedeschi before him — felt betrayed? Luckily, Chris and his family loved it — and nearly a thousand people posted messages on the internet forum saying much the same thing.

My own life underwent a change of direction not long after filming Chris Jarrett's fairytale story when I discovered I was pregnant. I'd wanted children since my mid-twenties, and suddenly here I was at the age of 31, unexpectedly pregnant only six weeks after moving interstate to start a new job.

After my son Oskar was born I took seven months maternity leave. I then applied for another position at the ABC — I felt trying to juggle the pressures and travel requirements of *Australian Story* — with the competing and conflicting pressures of motherhood would be impossible. I held this other position for less than a year before approaching Deb Fleming about the possibility of returning to the program. She agreed but just six weeks later I fell pregnant again!

It was during this time that I produced a story that covered a subject no parent wants to contemplate – the loss of a child.

While I'd been overseas filming Chris Jarrett's story, Vanessa Gorman, also a producer on *Australian Story*, had given birth to a little girl called Layla. Tragically, Layla was critically ill at birth and died soon after. Vanessa made a documentary about the experience called 'Losing Layla'. I had watched it just months after Oskar was born and, like thousands of others, it made me realise once again just how privileged I was to have a healthy child.

Now Vanessa was pregnant again and, after much soul-searching, had decided to do a story on *Australian Story*. She came to my house one afternoon and asked me to do the interview and help her put the story together.

I interviewed Vanessa late in her pregnancy with Raphael. Tears streamed down my face through most of the interview, and I know cameraman Anthony Sines and soundman Marc Smith were also crying.

We went to Sydney on the day of Vanessa's caesarean to film Raphael's birth. The theatre nurse allowed Quentin Davis and Ross Byrne (camera and sound) into the operating room, but my presence was seen as unnecessary. I had to wait outside with Vanessa's family.

We waited and waited, trying not to seem too worried, unaware that the hospital staff were having problems with the level of anaesthesia. Finally Vanessa emerged with her little boy. He was perfect. As soon as Vanessa saw her family the tears of joy and relief appeared.

Deb Fleming said something recently which struck a chord: sometimes people are very revealing; sometimes less so. There are the white bits of their life that they will share happily; the grey that they feel uncertain about allowing you to know; and the black that you will probably never hear about. With a friend, however, you often know about the black!

When I heard Raphael's father, James, bemoaning just weeks after the birth that he had ended up with a woman who constantly wore flannelette pyjamas, as a friend and feminist I was offended but as a producer I was excited. Here was a 'real' picture of motherhood: a sleep-deprived, teary woman without the perfectly ironed white linen outfit which mothers always seem to swan around in in the sanitised world of television commercials.

'Regarding Raphael' was one of the most difficult edits I've ever sat through because the first third of the program was about Layla's death. Normally, it takes an hour to edit a one-minute news story, so that gives you some idea of the time it takes to edit a longer piece. With the quality of pictures and sound demanded of *Australian Story*, the process takes longer still. So Vanessa and I sat in the back of the small darkened edit room for hours on end watching Layla's last minutes. Vanessa and I were both crying, and at one stage I turned to her and we quietly hugged. Editor Roger Carter offered to finish this part of the edit alone, but we both felt the need to stay.

Soon after this story I produced a story which was draining but in a completely different way.

Julie Gilbert, a former swimmer was one of three women who had provided information to police about their dealings with swim coach Scott Volkers. He was subsequently charged with indecently assaulting the women when they were teenagers. Under controversial circumstances the Queensland Director of Public Prosecutions dropped the case, denying the women their day in court. Much was said by former swimmers, lawyers and commentators in the media, and Julie Gilbert believed that she had been cast as a liar.

She went public, denying the allegations were spurious or motivated by spite. Executive Producer Deb Fleming felt that it was worth investigating this woman who had faced such an onslaught of criticism. Rather than accepting it, she fronted her critics head on and publicly 'outed' herself.

The program's researcher David Shankey made initial contact with Julie and then I went to her home. I spent weeks speaking to Julie and others before *Australian Story* decided to undertake what was a very risky program with moral and legal complexities.

Julie sat down to an interview with me and recalled her memories of the massages that Scott Volkers performed on her. Telling me was only the second time in her life that she had given a full account of what she claims happened. The first time had been to the police. I cannot tell you how impressed I was by her bravery.

The story aired in February 2002 and it changed how many people viewed Julie Gilbert.

A week later my daughter Monet was born.

Another program that will never leave me is the story of Daniel Morcombe.

Daniel was two weeks off his fourteenth birthday on the Sunday he headed to the shops to buy a Christmas present for his mum. The bus he was planning to catch had broken down and he was last seen standing on the side of a busy highway in Queensland's Sunshine Coast hinterland. Police realised very quickly that Daniel has been abducted from the roadside. That December day was the last time Daniel's family saw him.

Australian Story doesn't usually cover stories that have already received a lot of media exposure. But I couldn't get the image of Daniel out of my head. Every time I saw his mother, Denise Morcombe, interviewed on television I was haunted by the pain in her eyes. I suggested to executive producer Deb Fleming that we could look into the community's reaction to Daniel's disappearance.

Thousands of red ribbons fluttered from car aerials and letterboxes — a local showing of support and solidarity for the Morcombe family — a red ribbon came to symbolise how much Daniel was missed and how traumatised locals were by the

The site where Daniel Morcombe was last seen.

crime. A special 'Daniel' fund was established to pay for banners, posters, bumper stickers and an advertising campaign to keep Daniel's face in the public consciousness. So that every day in Australia, someone would see Daniel's face or name and perhaps remember something that might lead to solving the case.

It seemed to me this was a story that hadn't been told — and, deep down, I hoped that with one million people watching, the program might flush out new leads that could help the police and the Morcombe family. Deb Fleming agreed, and ABC journalist Kirstin Murray and I worked on the story together.

I'll never forget walking into the Morcombes' home. What do you say to a family traumatised by such a loss? There are no words that can convey your feelings; and no way your feelings can match the reality of the horror they live with each day.

We asked extraordinary things of the Morcombes, including filming those special mementos that every parent collects, from Daniel's first paintings to the last card he ever gave his mum.

'Into Thin Air' was broadcast on 19 April 2004. It was the first of my programs that my partner, Rodney, didn't watch. He just couldn't face it. But the day after it was shown, he tied red ribbons to our car aerial and letterbox.

I was touched that the Morcombe family asked the *Australian Story* team to the service they held on the anniversary of Daniel's disappearance. We were the only media invited.

Since then, a $250,000 reward and possible indemnity from prosecution has been offered.

The hunt to catch Daniel's abductor continues and there is something small that everyone can do in this case — tie a red ribbon around your letterbox or car aerial and send a message to the Morcombe family — and the person or people who took Daniel — that he has not been forgotten.

Early this year one of the guards at the ABC in Brisbane stopped me as I approached the entry gates. I was expecting a reprimand as I hadn't yet put on my identity tag.

As I hunted madly in my overstuffed handbag the guard said, 'You work on *Australian Story*, don't you?'

'Yes,' I replied.

The guard showed absolutely no interest in my ID; instead, with the passion of a religious convert, she told me how the previous night she had watched *Australian Story* for the very first time and she'd loved it. 'I'll be telling all my friends to watch,' she said. Carol now counts herself as one of the program's loyal following, and my routine on Tuesday morning always involves a visit to the security guardhouse to get her 'review'.

On *Australian Story* we often witness people revealing parts of their lives that they have never shared in detail, even with their closest friends and family. It is a real measure of how the program is viewed that people trust us with these intimate matters — and it's a position I never take for granted.

My job gives me a window into a multitude of worlds, and an opportunity to meet amazing people who are willing to reveal their strengths and weaknesses. I often wonder where I would be if *Australian Story* had never been made. I'm sure it would be less challenging, less worthwhile, less life-changing than the path I'm travelling now.

Tony Cooke, son of serial killer Eric Edgar Cooke, with Jack Anderson, the father of one of Cooke's alleged victims, Rosemary Anderson. They are pictured after a restorative justice conference, shortly after John Button, who was wrongly convicted of killing Rosemary, was exonerated.

Murder He Wrote

Wendy Page

In 1998, when producer Wendy Page embarked on a story about the son of serial killer Eric Edgar Cooke, she had no idea that she would become entangled over the next four years in one of the most notorious cases in Western Australian legal history, or that she would be drawn into a role way beyond her normal brief as a journalist.

'Murder He Wrote' went to air in July and August 2002 as *Australian Story*'s first ever two-part program. It was two years in the making.

The perennial question put to anyone working on *Australian Story* is 'How do you find your stories?' Well – in all sorts of ways. We hear things, we read things and people tip us off. We also expressly target people or events making headlines to get the untold personal stories behind those headlines. Often one story leads to another. In 1998 I embarked on a story that led me on a four-year journey, through a trio of tales, culminating in the most emotionally harrowing story of my career. It involved the families of a serial killer, a wrongfully convicted man and a murdered woman.

At the height of the great waterfront dispute in 1998, a Western Australian trade union leader, Tony Cooke, was making headlines in Perth. A woman from a previous story wrote to me suggesting he might make a good story. She had an idea that he was the son of the notorious serial killer Eric Edgar Cooke, who in 1963 had the city of Perth paralysed with fear as he murdered people at random over a seven-month period. It began with a killing spree on Australia Day. A married man with seven children, he was the last man to hang in Western Australia. He was hanged in 1964.

Tony was Eric Cooke's son and amazingly he did agree to tell his story. It was a brave decision. Eric Cooke was one of the most feared and reviled men in Western Australian history. But Tony's mother Sally Cooke had told him when he was a young child never to hide his skeletons in the cupboard 'or one day they'll jump out and bite you'.

'Sins of the Father', was broadcast in July 1998. Tony and his mother inspired enormous compassion and viewers were deeply moved. It had a profound impact on me too: you can't do a story like this and not get close to the people who entrust you with it and Tony and I remain good friends. But the story didn't end there.

When I was in Perth researching Tony's story, I was referred to a journalist, Estelle Blackburn, who was writing a book about Eric Cooke's criminal history, in an attempt to prove that a man called John Button had been wrongfully convicted for a murder that Eric Cooke had insisted, until the minute he hanged, that he had committed.

On 9 February 1963, two weeks after Eric Cooke's first killing spree, John Button was celebrating his nineteenth birthday with his girlfriend, Rosemary Anderson. They had an argument and Rosemary stomped out. As she walked home, she was hit by a vehicle. Button, following in his car minutes later, found her on the side of the road. Despite his efforts to get medical help, she died a few hours later.

The police immediately suspected Button had killed Rosemary. He was on the scene; they'd had an argument (which provided a motive) and his car was damaged from a minor accident four weeks earlier when he'd bumped into the back of another car. Before the night was out, John Button had confessed and was charged with wilful murder. Despite the lack of any forensic evidence to link his car to the murder, he was convicted of manslaughter and sentenced to ten years hard labour.

Four months later, Eric Cooke was apprehended and his reign of terror ended. He wrote detailed confessions to every one of his crimes, including the hit-and-run murder of Rosemary Anderson.

On this evidence, Button appealed his conviction all the way to the High Court, without success. Cooke's confession was dismissed as the attempt of a pathological liar to gain greater notoriety.

Button was released after five years, but was burdened with depression and the inherent emotional traumas and ramifications that come with a criminal conviction. For example, when his mother was dying in England, he was unable to visit her because of his criminal record.

For decades Button had protested his innocence claiming his 'confession' had been bashed out of him. Nobody believed him until Estelle Blackburn came along. Estelle was inclined not to believe Button either, but on looking into the case was shocked to discover that Cooke had attempted to murder seven other women by deliberately running them down — a fact virtually unknown to the public. Given Cooke's propensity for hit-and-run, there was a fair chance he'd also run down Rosemary Anderson.

Estelle spent the next six years researching her book. The evidence she unearthed was so compelling that I was persuaded that Button was very likely an innocent man. I knew it was a story for us.

In October 1998, 'Dancing With Strangers' went to air, timed to coincide with the launch of Estelle's book *Broken Lives*, which was published by Bret Christian, owner and editor of the *Post* newspaper. He too was persuaded that Button was most likely innocent.

The story brought several new witnesses to light, and one of Perth's leading QCs Tom Percy and lawyer Jonathan Davies offered to act pro bono for John Button. Most significantly, a former Scotland Yard motor vehicle accident expert emerged offering to help. Looking at old police photos of John's damaged Simca (the car he was supposed to have used to kill Rosemary), he asserted the damage to the front of John's car was not consistent with having hit a pedestrian. Unfortunately this expert was a consultant to the Western Australian police so he was unable to act for the defence, but at least he had alerted the team of Button supporters to the possibility of new forensic evidence.

John Button and his family were euphoric. At last people were listening and he might finally be exonerated. Eventually, the Western Australian government was forced to re-open the case, thirty-seven years after the event.

Bret Christian found Rusty Haight, the world's top car-crash test expert, who agreed to fly out from Texas to conduct forensic tests if three Simcas identical to the one Button had owned in 1963 could be found.

I was convinced this historic appeal was another opportunity for us, but *Australian Story*'s executive producer, Deb Fleming, vetoed it. No more programs about Button and Cooke! We'd lifted the lid on the story; now let others follow it up. But there was no way I was going to let it go. I'd become part of a team of journalists and lawyers fighting to clear Button's name. *Australian Story* had the inside running – why would I hand it over to someone else?

What if I followed the appeal from the perspective of all three families whose lives had been shattered by this crime — the

Buttons, the Cookes and the Andersons? Deb relented, but only if I could get all three families on board.

The Buttons and Cookes would be no problem — they'd been happy with my two previous stories — but the Andersons had refused to speak to anyone. I had already met Jack Anderson, Rosemary's father, when I approached him to participate in 'Dancing with Strangers'. It was a sad and difficult meeting and although I felt we had parted with affection, Jack declined to contribute to the program: it was too traumatic. They despised Estelle Blackburn for arguing Button's case in her book and nothing would ever persuade them that Button was innocent. They could not suddenly deny a truth that had defined their lives for so long. Now, eighteen months after the first *Australian Story* program about John Button, I had to find a way to approach the Andersons again.

Jack Anderson was understandably shocked when I called him again, but we agreed to meet at his daughter's home. Here I found Jack, his wife Joan, their daughter Helen, son-in-law, and teenage grandsons waiting for me, all seething with rage at my intrusion into their lives.

I managed to calm them down, explaining that I realised how terrible it must be for them to feel all that pain and anger again, but I couldn't put something to air without the courtesy of informing them first. The story would be widely reported anyway, so they should have an equal opportunity to present their side of the story.

Jack finally agreed. Then the whole family decided to participate as well. I now had exclusive access to everything and everybody involved in John Button's appeal.

We began filming in February 2000 when the crash tests took place. Button's defence team had a film crew there as well. This was vital fresh evidence.

One by one, Rusty Haight slammed three Simcas into a dummy that represented Rosemary. It was realistic and gruesome to watch. As anticipated, the tests proved that the damage to the front of Button's car was entirely inconsistent with hitting a pedestrian.

John Button inspects the three Simcas after the crash tests. All three cars bore identical dents on the bonnet; there was no such damage to his car in 1963.

Rusty then carried out the same procedure with a Holden, an exact replica of the car Cooke said he used to kill Rosemary. The damage to the Holden was identical to Cooke's detailed description in his confession and his description of what happened to Rosemary when he 'drove the car straight at her', matched exactly what happened to the dummy.

During that week, John Button's legal team released the results and footage of the crash tests to the media, hoping the Crown would concede that Button was innocent and quash Button's conviction. 'COOKE DID IT', the headline screamed in *The West Australian*, accompanied by photos of the dummy being tossed into the air over the top of the Holden.

The Andersons had no warning. Jack thought he was having a heart attack when he arrived at the newsagent to buy the paper. That night the family was shattered when confronted with footage of the crash tests — a re-enactment of their daughter's murder — on television.

I resolved then to warn the Andersons about any developments in the case. Nobody else did. Even though they were the parents of the murdered girl, the Crown had never told the Andersons that the case was being re-opened or explained why. They were deeply hurt.

My interview with Jack was harrowing. At one point he was so grief-stricken that I stopped the interview and we had a cup of tea and wept together before carrying on. When the interview was over, Jack said, 'Thank you so much for that interview. I seem to be feeling so much better for it. It's like a ton of bricks has fallen off my shoulders.' It was the first time he'd had a chance to be heard.

Meanwhile, I had to work on other stories. By chance I was assigned to a story about a former cop from Wagga Wagga, Terry

O'Connell. O'Connell is world renowned for his work in 'restorative justice', where he brings victims of crime face to face with their perpetrators.

I was filming with him in England where his work is very highly regarded. It was March 2000 and I had just come from Perth after filming the crash tests, and interviewing all the parties in the Button story. As we were driving through the countryside around Oxford, I told him about the case and how the Anderson family couldn't accept that John Button may be innocent. Yet even more than exoneration, John wanted the Andersons to acknowledge that he hadn't killed Rosemary. If ever he could help, Terry offered, he would be happy to do so.

A year later, in May 2001, John Button's appeal was heard. I kept the Andersons informed of everything that was happening in court. It was an extremely traumatic time for them.

By a stroke of good luck, Terry O'Connell happened to be in town working with the Western Australian police. I took the opportunity to introduce him to the Andersons. Jack and Joan were thrilled. They adored Terry. He made them laugh, and it was wonderful because they were so alone with their grief. Everybody seemed to be batting for John Button but at least they had two allies in Terry and me.

Nine months later the Western Australian Court of Criminal Appeal finally handed down its decision. On 25 February 2002, John Button was exonerated. All three judges agreed that his conviction was 'unsafe and unsatisfactory on the ground that there has been a miscarriage of justice'. Chief Justice David Malcolm even went so far as to say that the similarity of this evidence to that in the cases of all the other hit-and-run victims 'points directly to the likelihood that Mr Cooke was Ms Anderson's killer'. The packed courtroom erupted into cheers and tears. The joy and relief we all felt for John and Helen Button, their son Greg and daughter Naomi were overwhelming.

Tony Cooke, his four siblings and his mother Sally were all in court for the verdict, in support of John Button. However, it was also very painful for them that their notorious father was effectively convicted of yet another murder. They quietly disappeared to escape the media frenzy.

I rushed to let Jack and Joan Anderson know of the verdict before they heard it on the news. I hadn't known that it was to be broadcast live on radio. I will never forget the looks on their tear-stained faces as I walked into their flat. Even though Jack had always said he was a sporting man and would accept the umpire's decision – this decision was the bitterest pill he could ever have been asked to swallow. It was impossible to overturn forty years of hatred for the man they believed had killed their daughter.

Jack and Joan Anderson were very traumatised on the day John Button was exonerated, so the next morning Terry O'Connell and Wendy Page took them to have morning tea at Rosemary's graveside.
Left to right: Terry O'Connell, Jack Anderson, Wendy Page, Joan Anderson.

Thank god for Terry O'Connell who was in Perth again. He was the very best tonic I could have offered them. That night I organised dinner for the entire Anderson family, and Terry, at their daughter's home. I knew the very worst thing for them would be to be alone that night while the whole of Perth (so it seemed to them) celebrated Button's win. Their sense of alienation was acute.

Terry was sure the only way Jack and Joan would ever find peace would be to confront John Button in a 'restorative justice' conference. I couldn't imagine this ever happening. Jack and Joan were too old and frail and it would be far too traumatic.

In the normal course of events I would have rushed to get the story to air immediately but I was in the middle of another important story so this one had to wait. Three months later it was becoming old news. I rang Terry and said, 'It's now or never. If you're still thinking of bringing people together, we'd better make a plan and work out a way to do it.'

That night the most amazing thing happened. Jack Anderson rang Terry. 'I just don't seem to be getting over it,' he said. 'It just seems to be coming up and coming up all the time. Everybody still keeps talking about John Button. I just wish it would all go away and leave me in peace.'

That was our cue. Terry and I headed back to Perth.

Terry's plan was to facilitate a round circle conference where all the parties involved could explain how this tragic affair had affected their lives. First he spent a day with the Andersons. By the end of it, they were ready to face John Button. I then introduced Terry to everybody else.

Getting John Button to the table proved far more difficult than I ever imagined. He had always expressed a desire to make peace with Rosemary's parents. But his wife, Helen was concerned for his welfare and was strongly opposed to the meeting. Their daughter Naomi was all for it. She had a need to meet the Andersons, even if her father no longer thought he did.

Jack Anderson was the keenest of them all. But his daughter Helen O'Dea was shocked and furious with me. She had told me many times her parents would 'never, ever, ever agree to meet John Button', and somehow Terry had conned them into it. 'My father has poor health.' she said. 'This will be too stressful for him. If anything happens to him, I'll hold you responsible!' And under no circumstances would she participate. I too was concerned about Jack's health, but he was more ready than ever and just wanted to get on with it. He dismissed his daughter's concerns. He was going to be there and so was Joan.

Tony Cooke and his mother Sally agreed to participate. They had never met any of Eric's victims, or families of his victims, and they were always keen to make amends, somehow, for Eric's sins.

Estelle Blackburn and Bret Christian also agreed to attend. There was one other very important person — Rosemary's best friend Laraine Garrett, who had always believed in Button's innocence and felt the Andersons had rejected her because of it. She hoped this would be an opportunity to reconcile with them.

We negotiated for two gut-wrenching weeks. I booked a big rehearsal room at the ABC for 4 p.m. on a Sunday afternoon. That morning I still wasn't sure that John Button would be there.

I rang Deb Fleming and told her that I was feeling sicker than I had ever felt in my whole life. My stomach was churning. What was I doing? Had I a right to be involved in something like this? I was questioning myself more than ever. Was I a journalist driven by the smell of an extraordinary scoop or was this story an important exposition of the far-reaching consequences of wrongful conviction? I had become a player in this story. How unethical was that? What might the repercussions be? It was terrifying.

Deb and I had discussed on many occasions the issue of 'crossing the line' with this story but this was a most unusual situation. I had been sharing the pain of all these people for four years. It was impossible not to get close to them in the circumstances and I was the only person who had the confidence of them all. Deb was satisfied that in Terry O'Connell we had a completely reputable, world expert in 'restorative justice'. What had happened to the Buttons, Andersons and Cookes was monstrously unjust. The system had failed them all. Exoneration had not brought peace to John. He was now consumed with anger that his life had been ruined and nobody was being called to account. The Andersons were still burdened with anger and grief too. This was a chance for some sort of resolution.

John Button rang and said he would be there.

Then Jack's daughter Helen rang to say she would come after all 'just to support my parents, not for any other reason'. And John's son Greg was coming too.

John's wife Helen chose not to participate — a decision I understood and respected.

The moment arrived. The Buttons and Andersons were about to face each other for the first time since the night Rosemary died. As Terry pointed out, this was not about reconciliation; it was about the chance to deal with unfinished business so they could all move on.

When everyone was seated, Terry brought the Andersons in. This brave, elderly couple shuffled into the room, not looking at anybody. Jack was holding Joan's arm. My throat constricted with emotion.

Terry began with John, asking him to describe that night when Rosemary was killed. Greg and Naomi Button explained how it had been for them living with this terrible burden all their lives. Then it was Jack and Joan's turn.

Jack Anderson was sobbing and telling Tony Cooke that he would never blame his father for murdering his daughter because he didn't believe he had. I don't think Jack really meant that. He just felt enormous compassion for Tony for having to live with being Eric Cooke's son. Joan broke down too and declared that she could 'never ever forgive John Button because he took my daughter out and he didn't bring her home'. She was unloading forty years of unimaginable pain. It was harrowing for everybody.

Sally Cooke was stoic, telling the Andersons she honestly believed her husband was the real murderer of Rosemary.

Suddenly, I noticed that Jack had taken a turn. The very worst thing had happened. Jack had collapsed.

I did not waste a second, I fled through the corridors of the ABC to get to a phone to call 000. I was screaming down the phone, never knowing panic like this before. I couldn't believe how calm the operator was.

'Could you give me an address, please?'

'It's the ABC, it's the ABC.'

'But could you give me an address please.'

'It's the ABC. It's in Adelaide Terrace.'

'What number in Adelaide Terrace?'

I had absolutely no idea.

Thank god Greg Button was there — a doctor. He took control and by the time the ambulance arrived Jack had come to. His blood pressure was through the roof and he should have been hospitalised. But Jack refused to go. This was his big day and he was not going to miss it for anything! The ambulance medics made him sign a release form and he took his coat and tie off, and we carried on!

Justice restored: a transformation occurred after the conference. From left to right, standing: Bret Christian, the Andersons' daughter Helen O'Dea, Jack Anderson, Naomi Button, Tony Cooke, Wendy Page and Terry O'Connell; seated: Sally Cooke and Joan Anderson.

His collapse was a circuit breaker. Tony Cooke and Bret Christian cracked jokes and suddenly the whole atmosphere changed. Everybody told it exactly like it was; how it had been for them for the last forty years. The transformation was miraculous.

The week before this restorative conference I had made an appointment with the Director of Public Prosecutions, Robert Cock QC. There was such a trail of destruction in the wake of this miscarriage of justice that I felt I needed to do something to help put it right. I believed the Crown had exacerbated the Andersons' grief by failing to inform them that their daughter's murder case was being reopened and why. Robert Cock wrote a charming letter of apology to the Andersons and invited them to afternoon tea. It was such a simple gesture, yet it meant so much. They told Cock about the restorative conference and how they felt so much better as a result of it. Cock then explained how the Crown had tested the evidence meticulously and the three judges were all agreed in their decision. Finally the Andersons understood and accepted that John Button's innocence had been proven beyond doubt. Well Jack did anyway. I suspect it's still very difficult, even now, for Joan Anderson to denounce 40 years of bitterness.

After all the trauma of the previous four years, I wondered if the Andersons might like to hold a memorial service for Rosemary to let her finally rest in peace. They jumped at the chance. There had been no funeral forty years ago, just a graveside committal. And Joan had not been there because she was heavily sedated at the time.

I approached the Anglican Dean of Perth, The Very Reverend Dr John Shepherd, who with enormous empathy, readily agreed to conduct the service at St George's Cathedral. It was the most beautiful service I have ever been to. Dr Shepherd's eulogy was so perfectly pitched – addressed not just to the Andersons, but to everybody who had been devastated by the events and fall-out from the crimes of Eric Edgar Cooke.

'Murder He Wrote' went to air in two episodes in 2002. One of the greatest travesties of wrongful conviction is that the wrongfully convicted can never be fully restored to their pre-conviction status. There are always some who cannot accept that the system got it wrong. But our audience was left in no doubt. John Button received hundreds of emails, phone calls and letters of support.

A few months later my editor, Ian Harley, and I won a Walkley Award for the story. I rang Jack the next day. He said he hadn't watched the SBS telecast of the Awards because he wasn't feeling too good. He died six days later.

Thanks to Terry O'Connell, Jack Anderson died in peace.

For John Button, with the support of his wife Helen, life is improving. He was awarded $400,000 compensation and he is in demand to speak about his experience at schools and around the state. That's something he really enjoys.

And as for me, I can't imagine where my life would be today if Jack Anderson had died that afternoon when he collapsed at the ABC. I would never have forgiven myself. In my ten years with the program I've had many challenging experiences, and there will be more, but every journalist has a once-in-a-lifetime story — 'Murder He Wrote' was mine.

Jack and Joan Anderson with The Very Reverend Dr John Shepherd, Anglican Dean of Perth, who gave a beautiful eulogy at Rosemary's memorial service, forty years after her death.

Vanessa holding Layla, the day after her death.

Regarding Raphael

Vanessa Gorman

As a producer on *Australian Story*, I am used to being
behind the camera, not in front of it. I love to watch
people's personal stories unfold. I enjoy bringing out
a sense of the universal message within the human
struggle of anyone's life, be they famous or an ordinary
person with an extraordinary tale. But the roles were
reversed and I became the subject of an *Australian
Story* episode, 'Regarding Raphael'.

The program was a kind of sequel to a documentary I made called 'Losing Layla', which aired on the ABC in 2001. 'Losing Layla' was a very personal video diary documentary following my struggle to get pregnant with a reluctant partner, the death of our baby daughter eight hours after birth, and the passage of grief that followed. Many people who saw that film wanted to know what happened next in our lives. 'Regarding Raphael' was part follow-up, part celebration of a new chapter and a new life. But neither film was easy to be involved with or easy to make. Not only was I exposing myself to public scrutiny, I was revealing an extremely private experience.

On *Australian Story* we work with a film crew of two — camera operator and sound recordist — but we still lug around a mountain of equipment: a large Betacam camera; lighting and sound equipment; monitors; the hundred cables and bits and pieces necessary to get sleek, high-quality pictures. During the 1990s a new technology emerged: the digital camcorder. It promised to revolutionise filmmaking. Small and relatively cheap, digicams not only put filmmaking into the hands of amateurs, but beckoned professional filmmakers towards a new type of film.

One of the keys to good documentary-making is how much access you are allowed to your subject. Intruding into people's lives with all the paraphernalia of sophisticated filmmaking sometimes makes it difficult to capture the candid, everyday moments. It's difficult for the subject to forget they are being filmed. What these small digital cameras lost in quality, they made up for in stealth. They were unobtrusive and non-threatening, and documentaries were emerging that were often personal and very intimate. One aspect of this new genre that particularly fascinated me was the video diary.

I came up with the idea of making a video diary chronicling my relationship with my partner, Michael, my desire to get pregnant, and how pregnancy, birth and the first year or two of a child's life affects a relationship. In a sense: how a baby changes your life. What made the story interesting to me — even though, personally, it was making my life hell — was Michael's reluctance to have a baby. Conflict is the stuff of story, after all.

'This isn't just about a baby any more,' I would complain. 'You're also thwarting a creative project.'

Michael refused to be swayed for my art.

Long before I got pregnant I started recording our life — or at least the domestic interior of our lives in the bedroom, bathroom and living room. It was my hobby project, squeezed in around professional commitments. I filmed on and off for the next few years, often annoying Michael in the process. For no matter how small and unencumbered, a camera still changes the dynamic of whatever it is shooting. Mostly, however, Michael was supportive.

In 1999, just after completing the *Australian Story* episode about Wayne Bennett, I found I was pregnant.

My life and my video diary documentary were suddenly on track and I stepped up my recording with gusto. Attempting to be both camera operator and subject was awkward, though. Eventually, I discovered what worked best was wasting tape. I would set up the camera at the end of the bath or the bed and let it run for the hour of the tape. It didn't matter if we fell asleep in the middle: it was set and forget. Little by little we grew to ignore the camera's presence, or at least to integrate it into our reality.

It was often an uneasy process lugging the camera into my doctor's office and setting it up to record my own check-ups. I felt narcissistic and self-conscious. But I reasoned that this was a universal story I was chronicling, and the people I had greatest access to were myself and my long-suffering partner. Secretly, I hoped it would become a film about a man who, although initially reluctant to have a child, would fall passionately in love with his baby and hold a torch for commitment-phobic men everywhere. Except that's not how things turned out. Michael's reluctance morphed into trepidation as the birth grew imminent.

I asked my friend and filmmaker Cathy Henkyl to film the birth. Somewhere deep down I was appalled that I was letting myself be seen in this most intimate of states, but at the same time I knew I had ultimate control over the footage.

The birth did not go well.

A long and difficult labour left me exhausted and dehydrated and my unborn baby in distress. After nineteen hours, an emergency caesarean was performed and Layla emerged covered in meconium (baby's first poo in the womb), some of which she had inhaled in her distress. A few hours later she was airlifted from Lismore Hospital to Brisbane, but died eight hours after birth in Michael's arms. It was simply the worst day of my life. A living nightmare.

Cathy continued filming the day after Layla's death. It occurred to me fleetingly that the documentary project had gone awry. But I was glad Cathy was there to record the moment: I dimly understood that these would become our memories of Layla's brief physical time on earth.

'It was simply the worst day of my life'. Vanessa and Michael with Layla.

A few days later in hospital, in the depth of my shock and anguish, I set up my own digicam once or twice and let the camera roll. Inside, I sensed a silent figure witnessing my demise without emotion. This 'witness' whispered to me that the documentary had taken a 'dramatic' turn. I feel ashamed to admit that — as though I kept filming while the napalmed Vietnamese girl ran down the road; except I was both photographer and napalmed girl.

I had spoken to Dasha Ross, commissioner of documentaries for the ABC, about my original idea for the video diary. After Layla died I sat down and wrote her a letter explaining the turn of events, and sent her a copy of the footage Cathy had put together for Layla's ceremony.

She rang a few days later. Watching it had made her cry. 'Put together a proposal quickly,' she said. 'I think we can find some funding.'

Only six weeks after Layla's death I found myself standing on a rainy street, handing the courier the proposal package and crying bitter tears. Only six weeks old and my baby was being handed to strangers who would talk about above- and below-the-line costs in relation to her existence.

At the same time, I knew what I had was documentary evidence of a loss not usually seen or well recognised in society. A death somehow perceived as less significant than other deaths.

In the months after Layla's loss, alienated in the privacy of my sadness, all I wanted to read were stories about other people who had lost a baby. I needed to make sense of my own loss. I was hungry for the depths of their pain, to know I was not alone; searching for clues to survive it. If a film like the one I was proposing had existed, I would have walked over hot coals to watch it. I wanted to share my story in gratitude for those I'd read; so that other parents who had lost a baby could say to family and friends, 'There, that's what it's like, that's how much it hurts'. The social activist in me also wanted to show what had been made possible for us with Layla's death. What helped. So that people around bereaved parents could know what was useful, what was ultimately healing.

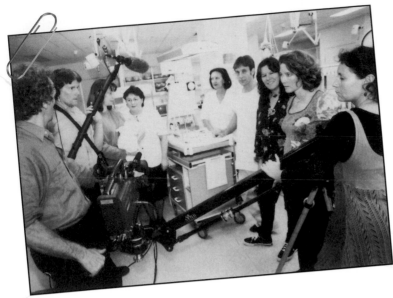

'I was standing outside myself as a witness to my own suffering, my heart split in the schism between subject and director.' On the set of 'Losing Layla'.

However, in a world of increasingly crass 'reality' television, I was worried about the audience's reaction to a camera intruding into this most private and sacred of places. It would have been impossible to introduce a camera into the raw environment of the hospital after Layla's death, but because it was already present, it stayed. Cathy was not 'crew' but a close friend padding about the room quietly with her small camera.

The process of making such a personal film was strange. I was standing outside myself as a witness to my own suffering, my heart split in the schism between subject and director.

I relived some part of the loss of Layla every day as I logged rushes, wrote the script and sat for a couple of months in an edit suite. The vision and sound mix were a spectacularly schizophrenic experience. My heart thumped at the sight of my daughter's dead body on screen, but the witness part of me entered into the discussion of whether a shot should be cropped or if we should up a sound effect.

I worried that in the process of making the film, watching my and Layla's story so many times, I might become immune. It did get to a stage where I recalled what had happened only because I was watching it on screen. It was too hard to go inside myself and remember what it felt like to inhabit my broken body and shredded heart. It was easier to see it on a monitor and experience it from a distance, like a stranger. Nevertheless, I found myself weeping through the final sound mix and I was glad not to be immune.

The gestation period of 'Losing Layla' — this 'second baby' — was nine months to the day of Layla's death. Sometimes, creating the film was my only reason to get up in the morning. It both helped me to grieve and distracted me from grief.

Michael was very brave, allowing himself to be seen warts and all throughout the pregnancy and in the aftermath. But if people watching it used the word 'brave' about me, I would blush and stammer that it wasn't the case. It was hard to explain without it looking like a shallow case of false modesty. What was visible on screen was my anguish, and that I allowed myself to be shown in labour, naked, sweating and vomiting. Later, my face crinkled with grief (the film was a terrible affront to my vanity). But what they didn't see — and what I was ashamed to admit — was the part of me that wanted all the world to feel sorry for me because I still felt so sorry for myself. The film was part social document and part primal scream of distress. Mostly, I was just a pathetically proud mother who wanted everybody to meet this baby I was in love with, to make her real to a world that would never know her.

I felt enormous trepidation before the film aired, as if I was physically sending Layla's body into the collective arms of a nation that might recoil in horror and say, 'Too much, too much'. I wanted them to see the reality of it, but feared they would be revolted by the sight of her corpse being bathed and cradled. Put off by a woman in the throes of grief.

On 1 March 2001, the film went to air on the ABC. We watched it at my mother's house in Sydney, with family and friends there to lend support. I wept throughout its entire length, noting its flaws, feeling my daughter's life being witnessed by the collective consciousness for the first time.

The online forum after the program was flooded with mostly positive responses, grateful for this glimpse into death and grief. People who had just relived their own loss of a baby thanked us for bringing the experience out into the open. But the greatest response was from parents who had not lost a child: they told us how they had gone into the bedrooms of their sleeping babies and children after the show and stood over them or picked them up and hugged them. They thanked us for reminding them of the blessings of their children's lives.

I felt so proud of Layla as, over the next days, weeks and months, emails and letters arrived from viewers thanking us for the documentary and telling us how it affected them. One woman wrote that the film had contributed to her decision not to commit suicide as she battled post-natal depression. When I thought of all the ways Layla had changed us, and what she had done in a wider sense through the documentary, I couldn't help feeling that her eight hours of traumatic life was like her time on the cross; her journey of sacrifice so that others could more fully appreciate the gift of their own children. Somehow, through her death, I, Michael and thousands of strangers could live more fully. The pride, the pain and the ambivalence around that feeling will stay with me forever.

Grieving for Layla and making the documentary kept me away from *Australian Story* for a year and a half. It was both strange and familiar to return to my old job as though nothing had happened: looking normal, making jokes, but feeling that chasm of grief just below the surface. I was lucky to work in a place where I could sense the love and understanding of my colleagues.

Michael and I had separated eight months after Layla was born, as he didn't want another child. In the interim I had met James who, although initially reluctant about children, decided it was something he could do for my healing. I was down in Sydney, filming an *Australian Story* on the actor Garry McDonald, when I found out I was pregnant again. The joy was tempered by inevitable anxiety.

When people heard I was pregnant, the question would arise: 'Are you doing a sequel to the documentary?'

'No,' I would say firmly. 'I'm leaving the cameras behind for this one.'

My boss, Deb Fleming, had also mentioned doing an *Australian Story* follow-up when I told her I was pregnant, but it felt too hard to contemplate. As if it might jinx things. I knew what people were asking for was a happy ending to a sad story, but

I felt irritated by this notion of happily ever after. How could there ever be a happy ending when Layla was still dead?

I had a public speaking engagement in my eighth month. Afterwards, three women rushed up to me. 'So many people were traumatised by your film that it would be beautiful to see something happy after such a sad journey. You owe it to us,' they stated bluntly.

Something about the conversation made me bristle, laugh, then relent. I knew if it was someone else's story, I'd be wanting a happier ending just as much as they did. In the end, I decided I could do it to celebrate this new baby's place in the world, and to make the point that having a live, healthy baby does not necessarily make for a happy ending. The loss of a child still lives on, no matter the joyous events that might follow.

Since I was working again on *Australian Story*, a half-hour episode with a team I knew and trusted seemed the right format. But I felt almost embarrassed to be calling attention to myself again. 'Losing Layla' had a purpose and a message outside of myself, whereas a follow-up seemed more like satiating people's curiosity about what happened next. I felt uneasy, as if we were characters in a soap opera.

My friend and colleague Claire Forster came on board as producer. Filming didn't begin until my ninth month: just a few scenes of James and my heavily pregnant self wandering along a beach, and an interview about the pregnancy.

Being interviewed when you're usually the one asking the questions is a disconcerting experience. While one part of my brain was articulating the answers, another part — my producer's brain — was ticking over in the background. *You're going on too long; they'll probably edit it back there. Oh crikey, you didn't put that very well; should I just start again or keep going and say it a bit differently? Bloody hell, hope my hair's not sticking out too much.* It was exhausting, but gave me great empathy for the people I'd been putting through the same process for years.

During the weeks leading up to the birth I felt anxious that the baby would die inside me, like so many of the stories I'd read.

'Hang on,' I would whisper, and was relieved every time it prodded and poked me. I felt as if I had been pregnant for years and still had no baby.

I'd chosen to give birth by caesarean at the Royal Women's Hospital, Sydney, needing the reassurance of a neo-natal intensive care unit nearby.

Once again I lay on a trolley waiting for an operation, but this time everything was calm. The familiar faces of the Sydney crew, Quentin Davis and Ross Byrne, hovered around us filming. These were men I was used to standing next to, working together. It was strange to be the subject, knowing they were just about to see my insides.

'Try not to get too much blood and guts,' I whispered to them. I suspected they'd probably ignore me.

We had a top anaesthetist but something went wrong with the epidural block and it refused to work. Out came the massive needle and another one was inserted. Time was passing. The block still wasn't working properly. I was beginning to feel sick with whatever drugs they were pushing in there.

They rolled me into the operating theatre, which was crowded with staff and the ABC film crew. My eyes rolled back in my head, I wanted to vomit, the block still wasn't working fully. I could feel sensations: the impression of my flesh being pulled and cut. I heard myself groaning. The anaesthetist stood by to knock me out if the pain got too bad. I wanted desperately to remain conscious for the birth, so I breathed deeply through the pain.

The smell of burnt flesh ... pulling ... tugging ... the baby high up ... being told to push ... thinking, there's just no easy way to get them out. James beside me, staring fascinated over the drapes at my insides. And then the whoosh as the baby is pulled from me.

I hear a cry, a kind of shocked bellow, and they lower the drapes and someone helps lift my head and there he is, pink and slimy and outraged, letting go an almighty howl as he is lifted and held aloft like the magnificent trophy he is. The sound of his lungs proclaiming his outrage is the most blessed noise. James and I look at each other and laugh with delight.

Then he is taken from sight and I can breathe out. James goes to be with him, anxious to hold him close at the first opportunity. The nurse calls out that he is healthy and well, Apgar's excellent (an Apgar is an assessment of a newborn's health, performed immediately after birth), and I can let go of the heavy fear that he would die within me and feel the relief. In the same moment all the echoes of this moment with Layla bombard me and I can't help it, I am no longer in control of any part of myself. I hold my hands over my face and sob into the cacophony that has been my heart these past two and a half years.

I got to hold him properly for the first time in recovery. A little bundle of newborn glory, his eyes lazily wandering, his mouth opening and closing with the first tastes of breath. James and I had agreed on his name: Raphael, after the archangel who comes to earth to heal.

As we were wheeled out, everyone lined up to see. My mother and sisters; James's sister; everybody crowding around to meet him. Upstairs, the tiny hospital room was jammed with family and friends, Claire and the film crew. The air was filled with celebration, with relief. I wanted to laugh and cry, to hold Raphael and sleep for two days straight.

This time, over the next few days, people arrived smiling and overjoyed, clutching useful presents instead of flowers. Everything was as it should be after the birth of a baby. Learning to change his nappy and bathe him. Learning how to attach him to the nipple. Waking through the night to feed him; cuddling a squirming bundle. I was filled to the brim with the extraordinariness of this most ordinary event.

And then life with a new baby began, and the reality of this miracle hit us with the force of a tornado. It sucked us up in its vortex and dropped us into the strange landscape of the newborn and their bewildered parents.

We were left to ourselves for a few months before Claire and the *Australian Story* crew turned up again to film us in the throes of coping with a colicky baby who cried much of the night and a good deal of the day. It was good to share the joy we found in him too: James had turned into the most doting of fathers, and I felt blessed by the salvation he offered.

In his interview, James was asked how having a baby had changed our relationship. 'Well,' he said, with the apologetic laugh of someone about to reveal an unpalatable truth, 'you go out with a sensual, intelligent woman and you end up with a frumpy, flanneletted, weepy mother.'

I laughed. 'Make sure you put that grab in the story,' I told Claire, because it was true. Flanny pyjamas were my new couture. I might be out of them by early afternoon, but by sunset I was eyeing them off again. Post-partum frumpiness comes with the territory. The hormones and the love leave you weepy and exhausted — and yes, I'll admit it, sponging vomit off my shoulder was the extent of my grooming regime. I scrubbed myself up for the interview though, and tried to look alert and sound articulate on four hours' sleep.

'I was filled to the brim with the extraordinariness of this most ordinary event.' Vanessa and James with Raphael.

The program was edited when Raphael was about three months old. Roger Carter, the editor, and Claire allowed me observation rights but completely ignored me whenever I suggested replacing a shot where I looked sleep-deprived and a hundred years old. It was also a little disconcerting to see my innards up there on screen; as I'd suspected, the crew had ignored my request and made sure they'd captured in graphic detail the climax of Raphael's entry into the world.

Claire and Roger skilfully weaved parts of 'Losing Layla' into the second piece. It was moving for me to witness a happier ending, but I was glad they allowed me my point —

that it can never really be a happy ending when you've lost a child, because that loss is always there. By then I was living a happier reality, though. Claire and I breastfed our children at the back of the edit suite while a curmudgeonly colleague from another program complained that the place was turning into a bloody creche.

'Regarding Raphael' aired towards the end of October 2002 and got another huge response. It still felt strange to see my private life broadcast like that, but the viewers' reactions let me know that it was for a higher purpose, and the impact of Layla's life continued to amaze me.

Shooting much of the first film with my own small camera gave me a greater respect and admiration for the film crews I worked with — the technical difficulties they face, the artistic heights they scale. And becoming a subject myself gave me the gift of a deeper sensibility for what we put people through in those interviews. I think I've become a better producer because of it.

I am now expecting my third child, a daughter, so have stepped back from producing for television for a time. I look forward to entering the fray again at some point, but back behind the camera where, I can tell you, it's a hell of a lot more comfortable.

(*Layla's Story*, Vanessa Gorman's memoir of her journey to motherhood, is available from Penguin Books.)

'I felt blessed by the salvation he offered.' Vanessa and eighteen-month-old Raphael.

About the authors

Ben Cheshire

Ben Cheshire was hired as an ABC News cadet in Adelaide in 1979, before moving to New York as a freelance journalist from 1986-1988. He rejoined the ABC in 1990 as a reporter on *Countrywide* and then the *7.30 Report*. While still working for the *7.30 Report*, he proposed an idea for the pilot of *Australian Story* in 1996. That story was broadcast in the first episode of the program, and he was offered a job on *Australian Story* a few months later.

The following year he won the program its first Walkley Award for 'Valentine's Day', a moving account of the death of a heroin addict. Since then he has also picked up a UN Media Peace Award for a story about the reconciliation of descendants of both victims and perpetrators from a massacre of Aborigines 160 years ago, the National Youth Media Award for his story on pianist Aaron McMillan, and a Logie Award (with John Stewart) for 'Into the Forest', on the family of serial killer Ivan Milat.

Brigid Donovan

Brigid Donovan worked as a newspaper journalist in Melbourne from 1988-93. In 1994 she began working at the ABC as a reporter on the youth current affairs show *Attitude*. She completed a trainee producer internship and worked on a range of programs, including the *7.30 Report*, *Four Corners* and *Lateline*.

Brigid began a producer on *Australian Story* in August 1997. After working out of the Brisbane office for two years, she is now the program's Melbourne-based producer. She has covered stories ranging from a submarine rescue off the coast of Western Australia to features on the rural rodeo and circus circuits. Other programs have included 'Carve Their Names with Pride', the journey of Queensland school students to Gallipoli and northern France, 'The Rise of the Phoenix', about the re-building of a World War II Liberator bomber and 'Boots and All', the story of the singing bootmaker, Peter Brocklehurst.

Deborah Fleming

Deborah Fleming began her journalism career in the UK where she worked in provincial newspapers before moving to the BBC in London.

When she married an Australian, she moved to Brisbane and worked as a reporter and producer with ABC News and Current Affairs. She transferred to Sydney in 1988 as a senior producer on Channel Nine's *Today Show*. In 1990 she became executive producer of the *7.30 Report* in Sydney. In 1995 she was appointed to start a new program that became *Australian Story*. Deborah has been acknowledged with a Walkley Award for Journalistic Leadership.

Claire Forster

Claire Forster started her career in 1988. For three years she produced talkback host Howard Sattler's program in Perth, during which time she won three national radio awards for documentaries and was named the best newcomer to radio.

Claire worked for the *7.30 Report* in Perth, Hobart, Melbourne and Sydney before relocating to Brisbane in 2000 to work on *Australian Story*. She was a Walkley Finalist in 2003.

In the past five years Claire has travelled to every State and Territory as well as France, England and Italy to produce stories for the program.

She lives in Brisbane with her partner and two children.

Vanessa Gorman

Vanessa Gorman has been working as a documentary director and producer of documentary television for twenty years. She worked as an overseas producer on the science and technology television program *Beyond 2000*, as well as various series for the ABC including *Review*, *Hot Chips* and *Living in the Nineties*.

She joined *Australian Story* in 1997. In 2001 the ABC aired Vanessa's documentary, 'Losing Layla', an intimate video diary about the loss of her baby daughter.

Vanessa lives in northern NSW with her two children.

Her written memoir *Layla's Story* was published in September 2005. (www.vanessagorman.com)

Helen Grasswill

Helen Grasswill has more than thirty years experience as a journalist, author, editor and television program-maker. She is *Australian Story*'s longest serving story producer and was part of the program's foundation team.

Many of *Australian Story*'s major newsbreaks — including Hazel Hawke's battle with Alzheimer's disease and Nick Ross's donation of a kidney to his boss Kerry Packer as well as the fateful interview with former Governor-General Peter Hollingworth — are among the fifty-five stories she has so far produced for the program.

Her most recent awards include a Walkley Award for Excellence in Journalism, a peer-voted Logie for Most Outstanding Public Affairs Program and the Human Rights Award For Television.

Belinda Hawkins

Belinda Hawkins has been a reporter with ABC TV and SBS for nineteen years. During that time she has worked as a foreign correspondent in a range of locations including Cuba, Far East Siberia, Nigeria, Eritrea and Germany. Her work has been recognised with a Walkley Award for excellence in journalism and eight mentions on the finalists lists, six in Melbourne Press Club Quill Awards, including the Gold Quill, and four United Nations Media Peace Awards.

She has a Master of Arts in English Literature from the University of Melbourne and started off her working life as a high school teacher in rural Victoria.

This is her fourth year working as a producer on *Australian Story*.

Michael Holt

Dr Michael Holt was born the eighth of ten children to Dick and Bunchy Holt in January 1960. The Holt family with its eight boys and two girls was one of a number of large families to live in the St Lucia suburb of Brisbane near the University of Queensland.

He was educated at local primary schools until Year 3 and then at Gregory Terrace, where there has always seemed to be a Holt boy and still is. He entered medical school at the University of Queensland in 1977 at the age of sixteen, graduating in the class of 1982. He worked as a junior doctor at the Royal Brisbane Hospital and trained as an orthopaedic surgeon at hospitals throughout Queensland, qualifying in 1990.

After two years of postgraduate training in International Hospitals in London and Europe, he returned to the position of Director of Orthopaedics at Royal Brisbane hospital in 1993, a position he held for six years before entering private practice in 1999. Dr Holt continues in private orthopaedic practice in Brisbane (after a small break!). He remains a keen golfer, junior rugby coach, father of four and all-round 'rugby tragic'.

Caroline Jones

Caroline Jones is the presenter of *Australian Story*. She is a writer and broadcaster who has been with the ABC for more than 40 years. From 1987 – 1994 Caroline presented on ABC Radio National 'The Search for Meaning' programs in which hundreds of Australian men and women told their stories of their lives. Caroline is the author of the bestseller *An Authentic Life, Finding Meaning and Spirituality in Everyday Life* (ABC Books 1998, reprinted 2005). She is an officer of the Order of Australia and in 1997 was voted one of Australia's 100 National Living Treasures. Caroline was raised in Murrurundi, New South Wales.

Matt Laffan

Matt Laffan is a lawyer with the New South Wales Office of the Director of Public Prosecutions. He was the subject of an *Australian Story* episode in 2001 and again in 2004 in a retrospective 'Where are they now?' show.

Apart from being a busy lawyer, Matt is also engaged regularly as a speaker and has a website that details his achievements and experiences in life (www.mattlaffan.com).

Rebecca Latham

Rebecca Latham started her career fifteen years ago with a degree in print journalism. She worked in commercial television before moving to the ABC as a television producer on *Four Corners*, *Lateline*, and the *7.30 Report*.

She joined *Australian Story* in 2001 for a three-year stint as a producer, covering a wide and fascinating range of story subjects.

Her work has been recognised at the New York Film Festival and as a finalist in the Walkley Awards.

She currently works on the ABC *Dynasties* program.

Wendy Page

Wendy Page completed her journalism degree as a mature-age student while raising three children and a husband.

After graduating in 1990, she began her television career with the *7.30 Report*. She spent six years on that program before moving to *Australian Story* where she's been since its inception — apart from a short stint on *Four Corners* as a guest reporter.

Along with *Australian Story* editor, Ian Harley, she has won a Walkley Award and been a Walkley finalist on several occasions. Together with Harley she has also been a Logie finalist.

Anthony Sines

Anthony Sines began work at the ABC as a trainee after studying film and television at Queensland University of Technology. He has worked for news, current affairs, drama and documentaries as a cameraman for nearly twenty years.

He worked on *Australian Story* from the beginning and has enjoyed seeing it evolve. He is married with three children and lives in Brisbane. He has won several craft awards for his work with the program.

John Stewart

John Stewart started out with a degree in modern history but was more interested in writing. So, with no real plan, he moved to the country and started working as a rural reporter. He ended up at the ABC in Sydney and spent many years working in television news and radio current affairs. His main passion is documentary film-making and video journalism. He particularly likes the idea of using small cameras and new technology to gain access to untold stories.

Professor Robert Tindle

Professor Robert Tindle received a PhD from the Institute of Cancer Research (London University, UK). He has been an active medical researcher for more than 25 years, in the UK and Australia (Adelaide and Brisbane). His research interests are tumour immunology, haematopoietic stems cells, and vaccines for infectious diseases. He is currently Professorial Research Fellow at the University of Queensland, and Director of the Sir Albert Sakzewski Virus Research Centre at the Royal Children's Hospital, Brisbane.

Awards

2005

TV Week Logie Awards

CATEGORY: Most Outstanding Public Affairs Program

WINNER: 'Into the Forest' – Ben Cheshire, John Stewart

The Melbourne Press Club Quill Awards

CATEGORY: The Gold Quill

WINNER: 'One Man Standing' – Belinda Hawkins, Mara Blazic, Roger Carter, Angela Trabucco, Ron Ekkel, John Bean.

The Melbourne Press Club Quill Awards

CATEGORY: Best TV Current Affairs Feature

WINNER: 'One Man Standing' – Belinda Hawkins, Mara Blazic, Roger Carter, Angela Trabucco, Ron Ekkel, John Bean.

2004

Human Rights Award for Television

CATEGORY: Television

WINNER: 'The Road to Tooleybuc' (Ian Skiller) – Helen Grasswill, Mara Blazic, Quentin Davis, Ross Byrne, Roger Carter.

TV Week Logie Awards

CATEGORY: Most Outstanding Public Affairs Program

WINNER: 'The Big A' (Hazel Hawke) – Helen Grasswill, Quentin Davis, Katy Graham, Ian Harley.

Victorian Press Club Quill Awards

CATEGORY: Best Rural Affairs Report in Any Medium.

WINNERS: Belinda Hawkins and Mara Blazic for 'On The Mountain'.

2003

Human Rights Media Award

FINALIST: 'The Cape Crusade' (Noel and Gerhardt Pearson) – Helen Grasswill, Quentin Davis, Howard Spry, Simon Brynjolffssen.

UN Media Peace Awards

SPECIAL COMMENDATION: John Millard, Ian Harley, Anthony Sines, Mark Smith and Robert Hodgson for 'A Bird in the Hand'.

ACS Queensland Awards

CATEGORY: TV Magazine

SILVER AWARD: Anthony Sines for 'A Bird in the Hand'.

SILVER AWARD: John Bean for 'With This Ring'.

SPECIAL COMMENDATION: John Millard, Ian Harley, Anthony Sines, Mark Smith and Robert Hodgson for 'A Bird in the Hand'.

TV Week Logie Awards

CATEGORY: Most Outstanding Documentary Series

WINNER: *Australian Story*

Victorian Press Club Quill Awards

CATEGORY: Best TV Current Affairs Feature

WINNERS: Belinda Hawkins, Mara Blazic and Roger Carter for 'Being Allan Fels'

MEAA Queensland Media Awards

CATEGORY: Best Feature/Documentary
WINNER: Claire Forster for 'Against the Tide'
CATEGORY: Best Cinematography
WINNER: John Bean for 'With This Ring'

2002

Walkley Awards

CATEGORY: Current Affairs, Feature,
Documentary, more than 10 mins.
WINNERS: Wendy Page and Ian Harley for
'Murder He Wrote'

New York Film Festivals

CATEGORY: Best Documentary Profile
FINALIST: Ben Cheshire for 'Dangerous Liaison'

Older People Speaking Out Awards

CATEGORY: Television, Queensland and National
categories
WINNER: Belinda Hawkins, Roger Carter and
Jo Bevan for 'The Quiet Man'

2001

New York Film Festivals

CATEGORY: Biography/Profiles
FINALIST: Rebecca Latham for 'Out of the
Blizzard'

Media Peace Award / UN Association of Australia

CATEGORY: Promotion of Aboriginal Reconciliation
WINNER: Ben Cheshire for 'Bridge Over
Myall Creek'

Human Rights & Equal Opportunity Commission Awards

HIGHLY COMMENDED: Ben Cheshire for
'Bridge Over Myall Creek'

Australian Cinematographers Society Awards (NSW)

CATEGORY: TV Magazine
WINNER: Quentin Davis for 'Inside Out'
Silver Award: Laurence McManus for 'Best
of Friends'
HIGHLY COMMENDED: Quentin Davis for 'A Sense
of Destiny' & 'The Battle of Bullo'

Australian Cinematographers Society Awards – Qld

WINNER: Anthony Sines for 'Something In
The Air'
SILVER AWARD: Anthony Sines for 'A Bug's Life'

2000

Alliance Queensland Media Awards

CATEGORY: Most Outstanding Contribution
To Journalism
WINNER: Deborah Fleming

United Nations Media Peace Awards

CATEGORY: Promotion Of Multicultural Issues
WINNER: *Australian Story* for 'Mild Colonial Boy'

National Youth Media Awards

CATEGORY: Best Television Current Affairs
Program/Documentary
WINNER: Brigid Donovan for 'Carve Their
Names With Pride'

1999

UN Media Peace Awards

CATEGORY: Best Television

WINNERS: Tim Lee, Mara Blazic, Kent Gordon, Vince Tucci, Erik Havnen, Ro Woods, Colin Jones, And Stuart Palmer for 'A Track Winding Back'.

CATEGORY: Best Television

FINALISTS: Wendy Page & Ian Harley for 'The Mango Tree'

Walkley Awards

CATEGORY: TV Current Affairs, Feature, Documentary Or Special.

HIGHLY COMMENDED: Wendy Page, Ian Harley, Estelle Blackburn for 'Dancing With Strangers'.

Austcare Media Awards

FINALISTS: Wendy Page & Ian Harley for 'The Mango Tree'

FINALISTS: Wendy Page, Julian Mather & Kent Gordon for 'The Long Day's Task'

Australian Human Rights Medals & Awards

CATEGORY: Television

HIGHLY COMMENDED: John Millard & Wendy Twibill for 'Every Breath You Take'.

Melbourne Press Club Quill Awards

CATEGORY: Best Rural Story

WINNER: Tim Lee for 'A Track Winding Back'

HIGHLY COMMENDED: Peter Drought for 'All Souls Day'

TV Week Logie Awards

CATEGORY: Reality Television

FINALIST: Australian Story

NSW Law Society Media Awards

HIGHLY COMMENDED: Wendy Page & Ian Harley for 'The Mango Tree'

ACS Awards – QLD

CATEGORY: Current Affairs

WINNER: Julian Mather for 'The Long Day's Task'

CATEGORY: TV Magazine

WINNER: Anthony Sines for 'The Scottish Doctor'

CATEGORY: TV Magazine

HIGHLY COMMENDED: Anthony Sines for 'Long Journey Home'

Acs Awards – Nsw

CATEGORY: TV Magazine

WINNER: David Maguire for 'Night Train'

CATEGORY: TV Magazine

WINNER: David Marshall for 'The Foundling'

CATEGORY: TV Magazine

RUNNER UP: Greg Heap for 'Home On The Range'

ACS Awards – SA, NT, WA

CATEGORY: TV Magazine

WINNER: Marcus Alborn for 'Dancing With Strangers'

SILVER: Marcus Alborn for 'Lone Star'

NSW Law Society

CATEGORY: Best Documentary

WINNER: Wendy Page & Ian Harley for 'Dancing With Strangers'

Australian Cinematographers Society Awards – National

CATEGORY: TV Magazine
GOLDEN TRIPOD: David Marshall for 'Tara's Choice'

National Youth Media Awards

CATEGORY: Best Television Current Affairs / Documentary
FINALIST: John Millard for 'A Place for Us'
CATEGORY: Popular Choice Awards
FINALIST: John Millard for 'A Place for Us'

1998

Peter Grieve Award for Medical Journalism

CATEGORY: Electronic
WINNER: Helen Grasswill & Sophie Emtage for 'A Cold Wind In August'

Rural Press Club Of Victoria

CATEGORY: Best Overall Entry
CATEGORY: Best Regional Story
WINNER: Tim Lee for 'Wally's Weddings'

Media Peace Awards

CATEGORY: Aboriginal Reconciliation Issues
WINNER: John Millard, Roger Carter, Anthony Sines, Mike Charman, Philippa Quinn for 'Camilla's Conversion'
CATEGORY: Multicultural Issues
WINNER: John Millard, Roger Carter, Sophie Emtage, Vince Tucci And Ro Woods for 'A Place for Us'
CATEGORY: Best Television
CITATION: John Millard, Roger Carter, Anthony Sines, Mike Charman, Philippa Quinn for 'Camilla's Conversion'

Walkley Awards

CATEGORY: Coverage Of Indigenous Affairs
WINNER: John Millard for 'Camilla's Conversion'
CATEGORY: Cinematography
WINNER: Laurence Mcmanus for 'A Cold Wind In August'
CATEGORY: Current Affairs, Feature, Documentary Or Special More Than 15 Mins.
Highly Commended: Wendy Page for 'Sins Of The Father'
CATEGORY: Sports
FINALISTS: Wendy Page, Philippa Quinn & Ian Harley for 'Winter Of Discontent'

MEAA Awards – QLD

CATEGORY: Best Electronic Feature
WINNER: Caitlin Shea for 'What Katie Did'

RACV Media Award

CATEGORY: Television
WINNER: Brigid Donovan & Jacqueline Arias for 'In The Line Of Duty'
CATEGORY: Overall WINNER:
WINNER: Brigid Donovan & Jacqueline Arias for 'In The Line Of Duty'

Human Rights Awards

COMMENDATION: John Millard for 'Camilla's Conversion'

TV Week Logie Awards

FINALISTS: Wendy Page & Ian Harley for 'Dancing With Strangers'

Australian Cinematographers Society Awards – QLD

CATEGORY: TV Magazine
WINNER: Anthony Sines for 'Bush Artist'
CATEGORY: Documentary
WINNER: Anthony Sines for 'Camilla's Conversion'
CATEGORY: TV Magazine
SILVER: Peter Moor for 'What Katie Did'
SILVER: Peter Moor for 'Alf Of The Antarctic'
SILVER: Peter Moor for 'Last Christmas At Kaloola'

Australian Cinematographers Society Awards – NSW

CATEGORY: TV Magazine
WINNER: Laurence Mcmanus for 'Cold Wind In August'
CATEGORY: TV Magazine
WINNER: David Marshall for 'Tara's Choice'
CATEGORY: TV Magazine
HIGHLY COMMENDED: David Marshall for 'Look Who's Talking'

Australian Cinematographers Society Awards – QLD

CATEGORY: TV Magazine
WINNER: Anthony Sines for 'Silent Nights'
CATEGORY: Documentary – Cinema & TV
WINNER: Anthony Sines for 'The Last Tentman'
CATEGORY: Current Affairs
WINNER: Anthony Sines for 'Her Excellency'
CATEGORY: Judges Award
WINNER: Anthony Sines for 'Silent Nights'

Australian College Of GP's Media Prize

Ben Cheshire & Sophie Emtage for 'Valentine's Day'

Older People Speaking Out Award – National

Caitlin Shea for 'Alf Of The Antarctic'

Australian Cinematographers Society Awards – VIC

CATEGORY: TV Magazine
WINNER: John Bean for 'The Last Muster'

Australian Cinematographers Society Awards – TAS

CATEGORY: TV Magazine
HIGHLY COMMENDED: Paul Di Benedetto for 'A Girl Like Alice'

Australian Cinematographers Society Awards – NSW

CATEGORY: TV Magazine
WINNER: Laurence McManus for 'The Good Life'

Australian Cinematographers Society Awards – National

CATEGORY: TV Magazine
GOLDEN TRIPOD: To Anthony Sines for 'Silent Nights'
DISTINCTION: Laurence Mcmanus for 'The Good Life'

1997

Walkley Awards

CATEGORY: Best Current Affairs Report, Feature, Documentary Or Special.

WINNER: Ben Cheshire & Sophie Emtage for 'Valentine's Day'

Australian Cinematographers Society Awards – SA, NT, WA

CATEGORY: TV Magazine

WINNER: Chris Moon for 'A Wing And A Prayer'

Photo Credits

Published by ABC Books for the
AUSTRALIAN BROADCASTING CORPORATION
GPO Box 9994 Sydney NSW 2001

Copyright © in each piece rests with individual authors, 2005

First published November 2005
Reprinted November 2005
Reprinted April 2006

ISBN 0 7333 1442 2

Cover and internal design by Nanette Backhouse, saso content & design pty ltd
Front cover photography by Newspix/David Kapernick
Colour reproduction by Graphic Print Group, Adelaide
Printed in Hong Kong, China by Quality Printing

5 4 3